# BLACK VINYL & WHITE SOUL

An Autobiography
By International Disc Jockey,
Singer-Songwriter, Richard Hallifax

# BLACK VINYL & WHITE SOUL

## Autobiography

By international DJ,
Singer-Songwriter, Richard Hallifax

© 2019 Richard Hallifax
Printing: BoD – Books on Demand, Stockholm, Sweden
Production: BoD – Books on Demand, Norderstedt, Germany
Layout: BoD – Books on Demand
ISBN: 978-91-7851-596-7

# A short introduction by the author

Thank you for opening this book. What you are about to read is an accurate account of my very interesting and unusual, but fantastic life.

My story begins with my young life in England where I was used, abused, and went through school with undiagnosed dyslexia. Then on to the world of British show business, including some of my experiences whilst working on the BBC TV program "Top of The Pops". How it was for me to work as an international Disc Jockey (DJ), and to meet celebrities such as John Lennon, Phil Collins, Elton John, and many others. I have included some romantic episodes too. Also the rollercoaster ride of life's up's and downs, but with the will to keep going no matter what. Why was it that I moved from a glamorous life in London to the wild forest in Sweden?

It is my hope through sharing my life's adventure with you that in some way the experience will enrich your own life. Parts of my story may even cause you to smile, so enjoy the read.

Richard Hallifax

# Chapter 1

## Born Again

The year is 1951; six years have passed since the end of the Second World War. King George VI was on the throne and Clement Attlee was the Prime Minister of the United Kingdom. Generally, the police did not carry guns and soldiers stood on guard duty outside the gates of Buckingham Palace (not inside). Steam trains, industry, and people burning coal to keep their homes warm combined to form air-pollution called "smog" that settled over London. In 1952 the great smog of London caused an estimated 4,000 people to die. Parts of London had not fully recovered from the German bombing of World War II and were still in ruins. At the time London was the world's largest city, and can you believe it, the pop-music charts had not yet been invented.

I was a home birth arriving in our house on Crofton road, in Ealing, west London on the 22nd of September 1951. I have heard that two midwives, together with my father, assisted my mother Lynette with the process of delivering me into this world. Of course, I have no recollection of the event, but evidently all went well. No one asked me if I wanted to live on planet Earth, but here I was – an innocent, newly-born child now in a world where there is a constant war going on between good and evil, and that I, or rather we, are caught up in the middle of the battle. Or perhaps I had been born again and had qualified for another chance at purification through reincarnation. In any event I was now here on planet Earth and this is where my story begins.

As a young child, or sometimes as an old person, one remembers very little, but thanks to my parents often recalling how family life was when I was a small child, I have something to go on. For example, one day I was left alone in the back garden behind the house on Crofton Road together with the family dog – a Cairn Terrier, who bit me on the right-hand side of my face. The event must have been traumatic, because Mum and Dad repeated the story over and over of what happened to me, throughout my life. Mother and Grandmother having heard my screaming rushed out, and seeing my face covered in blood, picked me up, and waited with me at the front door of the house for my father to come home. Why they decided to wait instead of calling for a doctor no one knows. But, it has been said that my mother's father did not trust doctors, so perhaps that is why. Dad arrived, and asking no questions, drove me straight to the local hospital. At first glance the medical team thought that perhaps my eye had been damaged. After having cleared up the blood they could see luckily that was not the case. However, I still have three small scars on my face where I was bitten, but as time has passed, they have reduced in size. Mum always said my scars made me look tough. As I like the idea of being perceived as tough, I don't mind having the scars! Another story that was told over and over, was when I fell out of my pram headfirst onto a marble floor, which may be the reason as to why I am who I am!

In 1952 my parents decided to move from Ealing and return to the area where they had first met. I will tell you how they met because it is a romantic, short story. Whilst in their late teens both where at a pond called Latchmoor, in Gerrards Cross, which is about 19 miles west from London, in south Buckinghamshire. My father had caught a fish, and finding my mother attractive he went over and they began to chat. I don't know what my father said, but my mother fell instantly "in love" and took fathers fish home and slept with the fish under her pillow! Now how romantic is that.

*Me together with my mother Lynette and my father Neville 1952.*
*Photo private.*

Our new home wasn't far from the Gerrards Cross area where Mum and Dad had first met. It was a small bungalow located in an area surrounded by trees in a small lane called Broken Gate Lane. Even though I was "knee-high to a grasshopper" (in other words, very short), I do remember the blue-bell flowers covering the ground in the nearby woods.

In 1954 my sister Nicola was born. Looking to the future with an expanding family Mum and Dad bought a larger, new house on Latch Moor Avenue, also in Gerrards Cross. This was my second move; one good thing was that my mother's mother, "Granny", lived very close to our new home. I recall cycling on my three-wheeler bicycle on the then stony road to visit her; it was always fun to visit Granny as she had a wooden rocking horse which I loved to ride on. The neighbours also had children the same age as my sister Nicola and me. They, together with our parents, came up with a modern idea (at the time) for babysitting, and invested in a walky-talky telephone system, so that both couples could hear the other's children when they were out, if we children awoke from sleeping. The idea was that if one of us cried, the parents of the other family who were at their home would go and check up on the children at the other home. This worked well for a while until our parents forgot to turn off the device, private matters where overheard and this caused embarrassment, which resulted in a breakdown in the relationship between the parents of both families, so the idea was soon abandoned. What was overheard must have been serious as I do not recall the friendship with the neighbours ever continuing!

Aged five, I moved for the third time, to another house. My family's new home was situated on a hill close to the village of Chalfont St. Peter, also in the county of Buckinghamshire. It is worth noting that both Gerrards Cross and Chalfont St Peter lie in the foot hills of the Chiltern Hills, and the two towns are also close to one another (2 to 3 miles apart), so friends and family who lived in either of the two places where never far away!

We lived in an area of Chalfont St Peter called "Chalfont Heights", named so because it was an elevated area accessed by a road that went up a hill. The name of the road we lived on was called Lewis Lane, which at the time was a winding, stony road with potholes that led up to our house situated at the highest point. From the second floor of the house we had a view overlooking the valley, and I remember how pretty it was at night seeing the lights from other houses on the other side.

When the move was being carried out some of my toys: a three-wheel bicycle and a toy peddle car, were offloaded in to the garden from the removal lorry when a small boy of my age came running from a house across the road and wanted to try out my toy car. He climbed straight in and I called him a "spoilt brat" and told him to "get out". Dad overheard this and I was severely told off. The next morning, I was sent over the road to apologize. The boy's name was Robert, and unbeknown to me at the time, this interaction was the beginning of a life-long friendship.

Robert and I shared everything; we played, slept over at each other's houses and did some things we shouldn't have, like stopping the traffic on the lane to make our own road improvements; we even dug more holes than were already there, and filled them with water! We loved watching when the cars splashed their way through, however, as you can imagine this was not popular with the adults who had to drive through the muddy water and then spend time cleaning their cars.

One time when we passed a red-letter box, Robert and I noticed a pile of tarmac that the road workers had left behind, and thought it would be fun to "post" the pieces of tarmac into the letterbox. At that young age we did not understand that there may have been important letters lying in the post box for the post man to collect. A few days later in the local shop we overheard two elderly women saying that the police were looking for young people who had put tarmac in a letter box; we were terrified and never did it again. Honest!

# Chapter 2

## *The Boy Who Could Not Spell*

My first experience of school was at a nursery school where I was left to play for a few hours a day on my own. Miss Beal was in charge and, as I recall, was a nice person; the nursery was at her home, but for some reason I did not like attending. My parents told me that I was "difficult" when Mother wanted to leave me, and that I cried a lot. But time went by and at the age of five it was time for me to take my next step in life. I was sent to The Holy Cross Convent in Chalfont St. Peter. A School that was primarily for girls, but boys where accepted up to the age of six. I have fond memories of the nuns, who favored us boys over the girls. At the school I loved walking up the path to a shrine that was called Mount Carmel. There was a statue of the Virgin Mary and I felt it was a good place to be as I felt close to God.

At the convent school I was unsure of myself because I found it difficult academically to keep up with the others in my class – in all subjects. I must have been nervous too, because on occasion I peed in my pants, and for reasons that I did not understand at the time I did not have any reserve clothing with me so the nuns would provide me with girl's gym shorts called "callots." Needless to say, I found these most embarrassing to wear.

In those days all school children in England received daily a third of a pint of milk. Each day our teacher delegated one of us to collect the crate of milk and carry it to our classroom. One day when I was carrying the crate of glass milk bottles, for fear of being late to class, I ran on the newly-polished corridor whereupon I slipped, which in turn propelled me into the air with the crate still in my hands and I went head first into a glass door.

The milk bottles smashed into bits and I ended up with pieces of glass buried in my head. I was rushed to the local hospital, the glass was removed from my head and stitches applied. Although no one's fault but my own, the experience was another reason for me not liking school.

The Holy Cross Convent School no longer exists but it was a school with a good reputation. In Gerrards Cross and Chalfont St. Peter lived (and still do) many film and television celebrities; one could describe the area as "England's Hollywood". Some of the celebrities who lived in the neighborhood sent their daughters to the Holy Cross, for example, some years after my time at the school the actor Roger Moore sent his daughter there.

My Mother inherited a large sum of money, which Mum and Dad decided to invest. First, they purchased the plot of land next to our house and then had an extension built with two bedrooms on the top floor, and a sitting room on the ground floor, which had a red-brick fire place as the room's center piece. The grounds were extended with a huge lawn and driveway, which had two entrances, all very grand, and to top it all off dad bought a new Jaguar car.

My year at the convent school soon passed. I was six years of age and together with my best friend Robert we began our time at a prep school called Thorpe House School in Gerrards Cross, a preparatory school for boys only. However, I do recall there was one girl – the daughter of a teacher. Dressed identically in our red and white-striped blazers, together with matching caps, grey short trousers and polished black shoes, white shirts and school tie, Robert and I were driven by our parent's and dropped off at the school to commence our first day. A teacher directed us to our classroom, which had small, wooden desks lined up in rows. We were told to "sit-down and be quiet". After being welcomed to our new school our first lesson began. I was terrified as the teacher walked in, she held a long wooden stick in her hand which she used to point at the blackboard on which was written the times table. This we had to recite the times table over and over until we could not forget it. One times one is one; two times two is four again and again. I can recite the times table to this day!

*Thorp House School, I am standing on the back row last on the left and Robert is kneeling on the front row second from left. Photo private.*

At Thorpe House school we were taught to play the games of rugby and cricket as well as how to swim. I was a good swimmer and discovered that I had a natural ability to be good in a variety of sports, often coming first in competitions. However, when it came to academic subjects, I was almost always last in the class. I found it hard to understand words and to this day have difficulty with spelling. Thankfully, sport provided me with a sense of achievement and much needed confidence.

At home Mother had suffered a nervous breakdown, which led to many years of illness and psychiatric care. This meant that Dad had to take care of the shopping, cooking, washing and cleaning. Leaving little time for him to concentrate on his business, the family, and the family finances began to suffer. The effects on the family meant that my sister, Nicola, and I often had to stay with family or friends as Dad could not cope. This situation continued for many years and probably was the reason why I did not always have extra clothes with me for school. The situation was so bad that my brother Charles (who was born in 1960) had to be left with a foster family when he was only 2yrs old. I remember the tears rolling down my face as dad left him there and drove home with me; thankfully his stay with the foster family only lasted for a month or two. Having gone through the experience of family being separated it was, and is, very important for me that the family is always together and united, no matter what the circumstances!

Despite all the difficulties Mum and Dad always managed to take the family on very nice holidays. Before Mother's inheritance was spent we went to Monaco in the south of France – very exotic at the time. Then for many years when money was short, we took holidays at Granny's caravan, which was parked on a site in the south coast of England, not far from the sea-side town of Worthing.

Christmas was always extra special; Dad had a way of bringing a "sense of magic" to the celebrations. He had been brought up in a place called Saltsjöbaden, which lies not too far south of Stockholm, in Sweden. Dad was born in Sweden because his Father was the Managing Director of the Svensk Engelska Mineralolje Aktiebolaget, which was part of the Shell Petroleum Company. Dad's Mother was Swedish; he had fond memories of his childhood in Sweden. We kid's loved hearing about the deep snow and the sled with Santa arriving with the Christmas gifts. Where we lived in England, he arrived by flying on his sled in the middle of the night, landed on the roof of our house and jumped down the chimney with the gifts. Amazing but true! If we had been "good", we may receive a packet or two, of course we children were supposed to be tucked up in our beds and sound asleep when Santa arrived, however with all the excitement that was never the case. We imagined that Santa had arrived by listening to every sound we heard and convinced ourselves that we had seen him!

Then, on Christmas day morning, we ran down the stairs to check out the packets that Santa had placed at the bottom of the tall, very beautifully decorated Christmas tree, which glistened with bulbuls and coloured lights. But before we could open our gifts, we all went to church. After all, we understood that we were celebrating Jesus birthday.

Once having returned home, after mass, we were then allowed to open our gifts, which we played with until it was time for Christmas lunch. Typically, in England, Christmas lunch consisted of a large turkey served with a sage and onion stuffing, roast potatoes, brussels sprouts and carrots, and the same was true in our house. On the table were also exotic fruits, dates and nuts. We each pulled a cracker, which went "bang" and produced a coloured, paper hat, which we each put on our heads. Later, in the afternoon, came sweets, pies and Christmas cake. But the best of all was that the family was together and happy.

Holidays and Christmas were amongst the happiest days of my childhood, but there was more, once a year Mum and Dad treated the family, and my friend Robert, to see Bertram Mills Circus at the Olympia venue in west London. This I loved so much that I dreamt of one day becoming a circus artist. For me the circus was a "magical" experience. I loved watching the clowns, lions and elephants performing, as well as the acrobatic artists who dived, jumped, and did the most amazing summersaults in the air; atop of bicycles balanced precariously on a wire high up over the circus ring whilst also being on each other's shoulders in order to form a human pyramid. To this day the circus is my favorite form of entertainment. The experience inspired me to organize my own circus in the garden at home. Together with friends, and by using whatever props we could find, including items such as Dads ladder, a bucket, and Mums make up, we dressed up like clowns, rehearsed our acts and put on a show in front of neighbours and friends whom we had pressed-ganged to come and watch.

We were also treated to another yearly event, and that was to see the Royal Tournament at the Earl's Court venue in London. This was, at the time, the "world's largest military tattoo". It was always exciting watching the soldiers and military bands as they marched with precision, and there were competitions between the different forces such as the Royal Navy and the British Army.

But then in 1959, when I reached the age of eight, an even better event happened. I was passing through the sitting room; the radio was on and a song caught my complete attention. I was "transfixed". I was stopped in my tracks and listened. The presenter announced that the singer was "Cliff Richard" and the song he sang was *"D in Love"*. This was the greatest sound I had ever heard, it was different, exciting and new, and from that moment on I have been hooked on music ever since.

Then, at around the age of eleven, I began to go through some very worrying experiences. Hairs began growing on my body in places where I thought they should not. "Was this a fungus?" I thought. In any event, I decided not to tell, or ask anyone, and taking a shower at school became a nightmare because I did not want anyone to see me. The other boys had no hair growing "down there", "why just me?" I questioned. In those days we received very little, even no education regarding the subject of sex, nor any type of information as to how one's body will change when puberty sets in. The only insight I received came from other boys of my age, who also new nothing, but made things up in order to "show off".

I was going through a very confused and worried phase of my life trying to figure out why I had hairs growing in "strange places". If that was not enough for me to deal with, my teachers and parents, who could not understand why I had reading and writing difficulties, sent me to meet a physiological "expert" to see if he could determine what my learning problem was. This involved me in taking an (EEG) test, "An electroencephalogram EEG test is used to fiend problems related to electrical activity of the brain".

Small metal discs with thin wires (electrodes) where placed on my head which sent signals to a graph to record the results which a man dressed in a white coat checked. All very frightening for a boy of my young age! I also had to perform problem-solving tests and I was asked many questions; my eyes and ears and almost everything else was checked too. Luckily this did not include the private parts of my body! Then, to everyone's surprise, the test results showed that I was completely normal for a boy of my age, but sadly in those days no test was made for Dyslexia, which is a general term for disorders that involve difficulty in learning to read or interpret words, letters, and other symbols, but that do not affect general intelligence.

Also, during my eleventh year I became seriously ill and had to spend two weeks in hospital. I was told it was Streptococci, in my case this was an infection of the throat and I was treated with antibiotics. As ill as I was, this was a break from school, which had become a nightmare for me because I was educationally so far behind in the class. At school I spent most of my time staring out of the classroom window daydreaming about running away and joining a circus or wondering about how God created the universe. No one had asked me if I wanted to be born, so why do I have to go through all this hell at school, I thought. I kept wondering that perhaps life on Earth was "limbo", a place in-between Heaven and Hell.

Because of the situation at home, with Mum being so unwell,

Dad did not have the time to focus on a job, or take care of business, Mothers inheritance had been spent, so times where hard. This meant that my parents could no longer afford to pay the mortgage on our house. With no other choice they had to sell our home on Lewis Lane in Chalfont St. Peter, and find alternative accommodation. Luckily a house was found that they could rent that was not too far away in the Gerrards Cross area. This was a blessing as my brother and sister where in local schools.

This was to be my fourth house move, but it turned out to be a good one. Our new home was a fantastic old farmhouse called Little Prestwick, situated not too far from Pinewood film studios; this was cool for us kids, because that is where they filmed the James Bond movies.

It was a big house and each of us three children had our own bedroom. Outside there was a stable block and a large garden that was filed with fruit trees, which provided the family with an ample supply of apples, pears and cherries. Family pets included a dog, cats and some chickens. One of the chickens had a name: "Henrietta" she was so tame that she often came into the house and allowed us to scratch and stroke her neck.

So, life was once again looking up. Shortly after moving in I noticed a young man leading a horse down the lane in front of our house. I decided to go out and take a closer look to see who it was; perhaps the young man would allow me to ride on his horse, I wondered. My sister Nicola and I, were very blessed to have a father who took us regularly to the local horse-riding school, so I knew how to ride. I gathered enough confidence and approached the young man to strike up a conversation. I asked him if the horse was his. "Gee yea!" he replied, I could hear from his accent that he was from the USA. "Hi, my name is Richard. We have just moved in; do you live here?" I asked. "Sure, my name is Chip", he replied. After a short conversation about the horse we discovered that we where neighbours. Chip explained that his family where based in England because his father was a senior officer in the US military serving at the US base in South Ruislip (as a matter of interest this was a non-flying Royal Air force (RAF) station, located in west London that was used by the United States Air Force (USAF) from 1949 untill1972 and later demolished in 1995).

Chip introduced me to a brand, new world. I was invited to the USAF base. At the US base I got to see basketball games, where the cheerleaders caught my eye! For the first time in my life I was attracted to the opposite sex! I thought the girls in the cheerleading team looked very sexy; they were dressed in very short dresses and looked very cute. I got to go bowling and eat real "American" hamburgers (it was to be eleven more years before McDonalds arrived in England in 1974).

I was invited to pop concerts and dances. At home I was often invited to stay for a meal with Chip's family and was, for the first time in my life, introduced to side salads. Chip's mother was very good at cooking and always made a tasty meal; at my home the food was simpler, such as beans on toast or fish fingers with mashed potatoes. Although I love all kinds of food, at Chip's house the food was something special. Also, during the day, Chip's Mum would provide us with a steady supply of cinnamon toast.

Chip and I started a music duo. Chip played the drums and I played guitar. He also thought me how to ride his skateboard, when in those days, in England, no one I knew had a skateboard, or even knew what a skateboard was, so the experience of learning something unique was, for me, all the more exciting. Chip and I had lots of fun and formed a friendship that has lasted to this day.

Mother being very unwell, and on medication, meant that Granny came every day to help with the cooking, cleaning and washing, as well as to help Mum take care of the family's newest member, my newly-born brother Ian.

# Chapter 3

## *The Boys Think You're my Sister*

In 1963; I had reached the age of 12 and it was time for me to leave my propriety school, Thorpe House. The question now was – which school would I go to for me to continue my education? Thorpe House thought that there was little point in entering me for the Eleven Plus exam because in their opinion I had little, or no chance, of passing it. The Eleven Plus is an examination administered to some students in England in the last years of primary education which governs admission to other schools.

Considering that I did not take the eleven plus, and therefore did "not come through the system", meant that my options regarding which schools would accept me where very limited.

There where long discussions at home with Mum and Dad. I wanted to go to stage school in London or to a ballet school, unaware at the time, that Mum and Dad did not have the means to pay for my school fees. I found out years later that they had little choice but to ask the local council for a grant to finance the next stage of my education. Regrettably the School of Dramatic Art, which I wanted to attend, was not the kind of school the council would provide a grant for. Neither would they provide a grant for me to go to a boarding school that catered for the normal curriculum.

In the area where we lived, almost all boys of my age at the time where sent away to boarding school. My parents wanted the same for me, never mind what I thought, so Dad took me to visit two boarding schools. The first school we looked at just did not feel right. In fact, the place gave me the creeps, and Dad agreed, so we looked at another, this time in the county of Norfolk, which lies in the east of England. Neither of the two schools appealed to me, but forced with having to make a choice, I decided on the school in Norfolk, mainly because the school had good sports facilities. The name of the school was Eccles Hall, a school for boys who found it difficult to learn in mainstream education.

I was very sad and upset with the thought of having to leave home. Then the day came when I reluctantly had to pack my large, green trunk with my new school clothes, which included green, corduroy shorts.

At prep school we wore short trousers until the age of eleven, then as a sign that we were growing up, were permitted to wear long trousers. At my new school, and approaching my teens, we had to start all over again and wear shorts. I found this to be very humiliating.

Dad drove me the 119 miles to my new school in Norfolk. For me this was a very long way from home and my happy life, together with my friend Chip. Dad dropped me off and left immediately, for the first time in my life, I felt completely alone. I found the nearest toilet, looked the door and cried my eyes out. How could my loving farther leave me here? I knew no one. When I finally plucked up enough courage to come out of the toilet I heard a friendly voice. "Hi, my name is David, are you also a new boy?" he asked. David had already begun to find his way around; he helped me carry my large, green trunk to our dormitory, which happened to be on the top floor. "We are not allowed to use the main stairs" said David, "teachers only; we have to use the small stairs at the back". After the long climb up the narrow, winding staircase we carried my trunk through the long corridor. The building was old, and so with every step we took the floorboards creaked under our feet. We arrived at our dormitory and placed the trunk on the floor. The both of us decided on which bed I would have, and agreed on the one next to David's. There were 12 beds lined up in a row down one side of the attic room. The bed frames and springs where made of metal on top of which was a thin mattress, the beds where close together, leaving just enough room to stand in-between each bed.

The school had two main buildings. The one where David and I slept during our first term is best described as an old manor house rather like Hogwarts in the Harry potter films, but not as large.

The other school building had a more modern feel and had served as a US Military Hospital during the Second World War. The two buildings were situated at each end of a long driveway, which passed through extensive, green, sports fields. There where tennis courts in front of the old manor house and a swimming pool near to the old US Army Hospital building.

Every morning we were woken by a bell at 6 am sharp. We had to get up and dress into thin, white, gym shorts; white vests, white socks and gym shoes. The morning run took place every day, except for Saturday and Sunday, in all kinds of weather, rain, snow, sun or thunder. This was followed by a lukewarm, or more often, cold shower. The showers had no dividing compartments and a male teacher often looked on. Then we had to hurry to make it in time for breakfast.

On day one we were introduced to the schoolteachers and other pupils. After breakfast we "new" boys were told to wait behind in the dining hall. A teacher then instructed us as to how to find our classroom. Once there we were to find a desk, sit down and wait. We did exactly as we were told. Having found a desk and a place to sit I turned my head towards the classroom door as a tall, male teacher entered the room. He was dressed in a long, black cape. On his head he wore a black cap with a tassel dangling on the side; and in his hand, he held a long, quivering cane, which he waved at us new boys in a threatening way. The room fell into deadly silence as the teacher slowly, step-by-step, made his way towards the blackboard and teachers' desk. His intention was to terrify us! And he did. Some boys broke down in tears as he waved his cane directly at those he randomly picked out. "You boy", shouted the teacher, and "what is your name?", "my name is David", "that's David sir", responded the teacher, "from now on, you will always address me as sir, is that clearly understood?" "Yes sir", responded a very nervous David, with tears running down his cheeks. Some years later we found out that this teacher was one of the masters at the school who sexually abused boys.

My school friends came from very different social and cultural backgrounds, some rich some poor. Some black, some white. A few came from as far away as Bermuda, Kenya, and Bahrain. We were of different faiths: Jews, Muslim, but mostly Christian, the majority Protestant and a few of us Catholic. We Catholics where driven to mass at a church not too far away, every Sunday, by the vice Headmaster who, before becoming a teacher, had been a monk. Despite our different backgrounds we all got along well. Because of this experience I have never understood why the adult world could not.

As you have probably gathered, I found Eccles Hall a rather unpleasant place to be. During the winter months it was so cold that we had little choice but to break the school rule of not going into the warm drying room. But we had little choice if we wanted to warm our hands. This we did by placing them over the heaters. What wasn't good was that this gave us chilblains and my fingers are slightly swollen, to this day, from this activity.

As young, teenage boys, we were going through puberty. But sadly, and regrettably, we had still not been given any sexual education. Consistent with my previous school some of my school friends pretended they were "experts" on the subject, but in reality, knew very little. There were rumors, such as "you will grow hairs on the palms of your hand" if you masturbate. To this day

I have not seen any hairs on the palms of my hands! During the night one could hear some beds being drown together as relationships between the boys formed. For some it was the need for company by simply holding hands, with others it went further. My school friends were not all young homosexuals, but through their normal development, and not knowing any better, found some comfort through being close to one another.

Sadly, a one-sex boarding school is the ideal place for teachers who are paedophiles to work in. And yes, some teachers had sexual relations with boys, and those boys became "favorites" in class. I longed to run away and tell my parents, but Mother was so unwell that I felt could not burden them with any more problems. Later in life I learned that children do tend to protect, or even "parent", their own parents when they have problems of their own. It is depressing to note that during the 1970s, after my time at the School, the then headmaster, Mr. David Tuohy, was accused at the Norwich Crown Court of 18 counts of indecent sexual assaults on five boys at the school.

My school friends and I made a mark on a board for each day that passed, rather like prisoners do in a prisoner-of-war camp. We counted down the days until we could go home. Apart from the summer, Christmas and Easter holidays there where half-term holidays to look forward to. Half term, unfortunately, was no more than a long weekend, around three or four days. It was my first term at boarding school, and I longed to go home for the half-term break. I was looking forward to Mum and Dad coming to collect me and take me back home. Almost everyone else had already left the school for the holiday. I waited for my parents to arrive. I waited so long I thought that they were not going to show up, but eventually they did. "Hi son, sorry we are late" said Dad. "We are going out for a day trip to Great Yarmouth – a sea-side town on the east coast of Norfolk", he said. I was deeply disappointed. "I thought we were going home" I demonstrated, thinking to myself how much I had looked forward to getting back home and spending time with my friend Chip.

My father loved boats, so when we arrived at Yarmouth we went out on a boat trip. I was miserable and hardly said a word. We went to a restaurant and then I was driven back to the school. I spent the remaining two days of the half term almost alone. There was a couple of other boys whose parents lived overseas and me in the large, empty, cold, school buildings. We had little to do except dream about the next holiday. I have no idea as to why Mum and Dad did not take me home that half term, except perhaps it was due to Mother not being well. Mum continued to suffer from depression. Despite Mum not being well she looked beautiful, and much younger than her age. As we said goodbye, I mentioned to her that the boys think you're my sister.

But Eccles Hall wasn't all bad. The older boys had a band and they were brilliant at playing music, they sounded just like the instrumental group "The Shadows", especially when hearing them play tunes like *"Foot Tapper"* and *"Wonderful Land"*. They inspired me to improve my guitar playing. One member of the band, Robin, took time to teach me some new chords. Robin was a school prefect, a title given to some of the oldest boys in the school. Being a prefect meant that he had privileges such as going to bed at a time of his choosing and having a room with comfortable furniture where he could make coffee, tea and toast. But, being a prefect came with responsibilities such as turning the lights off at night in the dormitories, being responsible for a class when they were doing their homework (which in our case we had to do at school), and making sure the rest of us kept to the school rules. Prefects also had the authority to send us to the head teacher for punishment if we did not do what they said.

One day Robin asked me to meet him at the back entrance of the school building just before it was time for the boys to go to bed at 9 pm. Robin had been very kind to me, teaching me chords on the guitar, so thinking nothing of his request I went to meet him. "What do you want?" I enquired, and then Robin asked politely if he may give me a goodnight kiss on my cheek and asked that I not tell anyone. I was 13 years old and thought this to be a big brother thing and agreed, so every night at the same time for a few weeks I went to meet Robin and he kissed me on the cheek. Later, I realized that Robin must have had a crush on me, but apart from the kiss he never made any other sexual advances towards me. This was, however, to be the first of many experiences of men wanting to have relationships with me over the years to come.

Then came the holidays when I could go back home, where I spent most of my time with my friend Chip. When I returned home I did so with the newly acquired ability to play more chords on the guitar, having received instructions from Robin at school. I did not share with Chip what a "hell" my school was, because I was too embarrassed to do so. I just loved coming back home where I could play and sing new songs together with Chip. If we look for it there is always something positive in the negative!

At school came a question "what is the definition of music?", asked my favorite teacher Mr. Turner. No one in the class knew the answer, there were some guesses, "it's a sound", "its rock" "no it's pop" different boys said. The best answer was, and still is, Mr. Turner's, which is that music is a series of sounds pleasing to the ear. At the time some sounds pleasing to my ear where coming from a group from Liverpool called "The Beatles" who, in the early 60s, had their first hit songs which included *From Me to You*" and "*She Loves You*". The Beatles had long hair, "The Beatle hair cut", although when we look at photos of them today their hair was in fact quite short. But I wanted to look like a "Beatle" and grow my hair long! However, at school we were forced to cut our hair short. And this was another reason for me not to like school.

*My cousin Malcolm on the left, Chip on the Drums, and me. Photo private.*

Every Thursday evening the school allowed us to watch the British Broadcasting Corporation Television (BBC TV) program "Top of the Pops". The program showed a rundown of the week's top music hits, which were performed by popular music artists such as "The Beatles", "The Rolling Stones", and "The Kinks", or whichever artist had a hit song at the time. For me, "Top of the Pops" was the center of the universe and I loved watching the program.

During the school holidays in 1964 I went to see "The Beatles" film, "A Hard Day's Night", at the Gerrards Cross cinema. On arrival to the theatre at Ethorpe Cresent, I was astonished

27

when I saw the long queue of people outside waiting to get in. Would there be a seat available for me I wondered? In the queue, girls where screaming with excitement. It was as if "The Beatles" where physically inside the theatre about to perform. Britain was proud of the four boys from Liverpool, who had become world famous. Traveling outside of the country in those days was unusual, but we had four working-class lads from Liverpool who represented our country, and that was something everyone in Britain loved. I dreamed of being in a group just like "The Beatles"!

As the long queue moved slowly towards the cinema entrance, I felt my heartbeat increase as the excitement and anticipation of seeing the film increased. I could hear the songs which I had listened to over and over; go around in my head, songs like "*I Should Have Known* Better" and "*Tell Me Why*", not to mention "*A Hard Day's Night*". I was lucky, I bought my ticket and walked the few feet to have my ticket torn in two by a man who stood at the entrance to the theatre, but that was ok because now I was inside and had a seat. It wasn't often the cinema was full, but on that day it was – not an empty seat to be seen. In those days almost everyone smoked, and as soon as the red curtains parted, and the cinema screen appeared, one could see "clouds" of cigarette smoke in the projector light beam as the commercials and film trailers where shown before the main film. In the back row there were always a few "tough guys" or at least they thought they were. They usually wore leather jackets, and rested their feet on the seats in front, "showing off" in front of their girlfriends, some kissing and cuddling, and some shouting and screaming, not because of "The Beatles" film, but to demonstrate that they were present and that everyone else had better "watch out". I was respectful of them, but somewhat terrified too. Just before the film was to begin the emergency door would open and one or two of the gang would let their friends in for free. Then, on both sides of the isle were girls dressed in short skirts and hats, who sold ice cream and chocolate. The trays they carried where illuminated just enough so that one could see where they were in case one wanted to buy something during the film. Then when "The Beatles" film started, once again the girls began to scream, "Paul I love you", "John I love you". I wanted to sing along as "The Beatles" sang *It's Been a Hard* Day's Night" but was too shy to do so.

As usual the school holidays soon passed, and it was time to return to Eccles Hall. At the end of January1965 the School selected a few boys to travel to London to pay respects to Sir Winston Churchill who had passed away. His body was lying in state at Westminster Hall in London. I felt privileged to have been selected. Upon arriving at Westminster, we joined a very long queue of people. It took hours for the queue to move forward but eventually we were inside the hall, and slowly we passed his coffin. We realized that we were witnessing a profound moment in history and that the person lying in the coffin had been a great man. The experience led me to believe that despite my reading and writing difficulties, I had been selected by the school for this event so they must have noticed something good in me.

I joined the School Scout group. In the woods behind the main school building was a disused building which the US military must have built during the Second World War, this we used for Scout meetings. Every one of us scouts had the responsibility to clean the building and when it was my turn I decided to do a thorough job. I took out all the chairs, in fact everything, and cleaned the place from top to bottom. The scout master was so impressed that he wanted me to take the test to become a patrol leader. This required knowing how to tie knots as well as knowing the rules and history of the scout movement. I knew how to tie some knots and some of the history of the scout movement, but not everything. A friend gave me some help during the test by holding up answers written on pieces of paper behind the scout masters head. The scout master knew what was going on and as the whole procedure was not taken too seriously, I passed and became a patrol leader. The lesson I learnt was that cleaning can get you places.

At school, discipline was taught to us to the extreme. During one term, every Sunday morning, every student in the school had to stand in line, and then a master would inspect our shoes. If our black shoes were not clean enough, we were sent for a caning, or if you were lucky you would receive the lighter punishment, the slipper, ether way it hurt.

Theft was very unusual at school, but sadly on occasion it did happen. When something was stolen and no one owned up to the crime, the entire school was punished. First came the collective punishment, no one was aloud out of the school grounds at weekends until the culprit owned up, and on one occasion this went on for a few weeks. Eventually, when the guilty boy decided to come forward, his punishment came, and it was barbaric. I recall the occasion well; all school pupils and teachers were instructed to assemble in the gym. The pupils were told to stand with backs to the walls and give enough space so that everyone could focus their eyes to the center of the gym and witness the horror that was about to take place. "Quiet", shouted the vice headmaster, then in came the headmaster dressed in his black cape; in his right hand he held a long, quivering cane. The guilty boy, wearing only thin, white, gym shorts, was instructed to go to the middle of the hall. Then the headmaster gave the instruction for the boy to bend over; the master drew his cane up as far as he could reach and with his full force struck down on the boy's bottom, not once, not twice, but six times! When the punishment had finished one could see the blood lines through the guilty boy's white shorts. Witnessing this made me ashamed of my school, and teachers, and contributed again to my hatred of the institution.

As had been the case at my previous school the one thing I was good at, apart from music, was sports. I came first or second in all athletic competitions and won the school Victor- ludorum twice, that meant that I was the overall champion in sports competitions, and my name was inscribed on the school honours board for all to see, in the dining hall. This was of course good for my self-confidence! But when it came to academic subjects, the difficulty I had with reading and spelling continued to hold me back.

If it wasn't enough that we school children knew that there were at least two teachers who sexually abused boys at school, we were to be confronted with one more, but this time a stranger.

During my free time I trained to improve my ability with pole vaulting, we did not have the new, modern, fiberglass poles, ours where made of aluminum, so I did not manage to vault great heights, nevertheless I was one of the best at pole vaulting at school.

I had just completed a vault when I noticed a strange man standing at the beginning of the runway and thought he must be a parent of one of the boys who had come to visit, so thought nothing of it. I carried my pole back to the starting place for the run up and said, "Hello sir". The man then asked me questions about pole vaulting. After explaining what it was all about, he then asked me what I was going to do on the following Saturday, to which I replied that I had no plans. The man then invited me to go out with him; he said that he would collect me at 10 am and that he would buy me sweets, which sounded great to me, as I would have done almost anything to get away from the school. Fortunately, it had been drummed into me from a young age not to talk to strangers, which of course was what I was doing, or to go anywhere with them. I explained to the man that I would first have to have permission from the school, and then he left.

A few days later whilst having lunch in the school dining hall the headmaster walked in. When he passed the boys in the middle row he would prod them in the back, he did this to encourage us to sit up straight, and as usual when the headmaster made his entrance, the hall fell silent, whether this was out of fear or respect, I do not know, probably a bit of both. The headmaster then asked us to raise our hand if any of us had been approached by a strange man. I raised my hand, but I was not the only one, several hands went up. He went on to say that as soon as we had eaten our lunch we were to report to his study, once there, we were met by a police officer who wanted a description of the man. We were told that under no circumstances were we to talk or go anywhere with the man, and that he was extremely dangerous.

We were of course terrified, but I thought to myself if they, the police, only knew about the school's own teachers abusing boys.

I have been asked as to why we boys never told anyone about the schoolteachers abusing boys, and the reason is that we were terrified of being beaten with the cane. Eccles hall was run like a régime, as long as we could be caned and punished, none of us dared to tell.

Every summer Eccles Hall held its major sporting event our own mini "Olympic games", but without the Olympic flame or anyone from outside the school present, such as parents and friends. The School sports day involved competitions between the different classes of the school. It was my second year at the school, and I was approaching 14yrs of age.

Sports day had arrived, and the weather was perfect, not a cloud in the sky, and one could feel an air of excitement as the entire school gathered on the sports field with its newly painted, white running tracks. As I approached the events area, my nostrils flared as I breathed in the scent from the freshly-cut grass.

Then it was time for the first event, the one-hundred-yard sprint, followed by javelin, and then discus. With each event the excitement of who might win caused all those not taking part in the competition to clap and cheer.

As I was good at sports I was among the athletes representing my class and I loved being cheered on to win in the various events which also included high jump, long jump, triple jump, pole vault and putting the shot, as well as the track events which included middle and long distance running. With each event the excitement among the competitors increased even more. Then, in late afternoon, the time came for the final event, which was the relay race.

I do not recall any other day when the whole school was in such a happy and excited mood. When the relay race starter gun went off everyone stood up shouting and cheering for their team to win. There were four athletes in each relay team and a baton was passed from one runner to the other at set places around the running track.

As the race went on, all of a sudden and for no apparent reason, the vice head master, whom everyone feared, began to scream at the top of his voice, "sit down, sit down, sit down, slowly but surely all the fun and excitement vanished, we all sat down in silence, then the entire school was instructed to commence the dreaded five-mile run. The five-mile run took place on roads out of the school grounds and was regarded by many of us as the "punishment run". But why now, why today of all days, when everything was fine, the only plausible explanation I can think of is that the vice head master had gone temporarily mad, he had completely lost his temper, why I will never know, perhaps he felt his sense of authority had been lost when none of us first heard his command to sit down, due to all the loud cheering and excitement.

Having no choice, and with a real sense of disappointment, we began the five-mile run, but as soon as we were out of sight from the school, the group I was in began walking, until a teacher came by in his car to make sure that we were in fact running. The routine was that those at the back, who were walking, upon noticing the teachers car approaching, alerted those in front by shouting "pass it on, the teacher is coming", then all of us who were walking began to run, then, after the teacher had driven by we resumed to walking.

I was together with some friends when we arrived at the halfway point of the five-mile run, and believing that we had been unfairly treated, we decided to take a short cut through the fields; this was something we had never done before.

Initially, walking through the fields seemed to be far more pleasant than running or walking on the road! The short cut took us first through fields where sugar beet grew, and then past fields where cows where grazing, so far so good, but then we were walking in what felt like swamp land, which just got deeper the further we went, soon we were knee-deep in what seemed like a mixture of mud and what smelt like shit. We then realized that we were in the middle of a sewage-treatment farm!

We started to question among ourselves how we were going to explain this. "Why we were covered in mud and smelling like shit?". Somehow we would have to get to the showers without being seen, but that was not going to be easy because we had to join the others who had not taken the short cut, in order to give the impression that we had completed the full run with them. This was important, because if it be known that we had taken a short cut, we might be caned!

Luckily the school master who was on duty when we arrived back was also dismayed as to why our sports day had been cancelled, he had a much-needed laugh when we had to explain why we were covered in mud and smelt of shit.

For me this was another of life's lessons. And that is: if you take short cuts you may end up in the shit!

One night I woke with a fever and was desperate to go to the toilet, I climbed out of bed and almost collapsed. Feeling extremely giddy I made my way to the toilet, only to discover that my testicles had swollen up to the size of tennis balls. In the morning I was not able to stand up and asked a friend to fetch the school nurse. Upon realizing that I had an extremely high temperature the nurse instructed me to go to the school sickbay immediately, trying hard not to disclose the pain I was going through when walking I made it to the sick bay and climbed into bed. Next to me was another boy who wasn't feeling well. After a few days my temperature began to normalize, and the nurse wanted me to get up and return to my class. But this was to prove impossible, due to the pain I experienced when I tried to stand up. I would have to tell the nurse about what was wrong with me; I thought to myself, however, I had two problems with this. One, I had no idea for the correct name for testicles. My friends and I referred to them as "balls", so I asked the boy lying next to me if he knew what the correct name for testicles was, "yes" he said, "they are called "Thyroid Glands"". So, I informed the nurse that my "Thyroid Glands" where swollen. After some deliberation the nurse and I arrived at the correct name. I was then asked to reveal my problem to the nurse as well as the headmaster. This I found to be most embarrassing.

The doctor was called and shortly afterword's an ambulance too. As I could not walk, I was carried by stretcher to the ambulance and driven to the Norfolk Hospital in Norwich.

I heard later that the headmaster thought that someone had kicked me in the groin, so he gave the entire school a lecture on how dangerous it was to do so. I do recall having been kicked during a rugby match, whether that was the cause of my problem I don't know.

During my first few days at the hospital I was x-rayed from head to foot, as the doctors tried to find out what was wrong with me in order to apply treatment. As it turned out I had an infection, and recall being treated with antibiotics.

The hospital ward was a long, large room with many beds lining each side. When the nurse and / or doctor visited one of us in the ward, a curtain was drawn around the bed for privacy. In the middle of the ward there was a desk behind which sat the duty nurse. During my first week in the ward the nurse asked if I was ready for my operation, no one had mentioned to me that I was to be operated on! I was of course terrified because in my imagination I thought they were going to castrate me. Later, I was told that it was not me they were going to operate on, but another young boy who was on his way to the hospital to have his appendix taken out.

Before I move on, I must share this story with you. One day the school athletics teacher came to visit me. Mr. Colman was young looking, and easy to get along with, so our meeting was relaxed. Mistaking Mr. Colman as a friend of mine the man in the next bed to me told him some dirty jokes. Mr. Colman looked most embarrassed as these jokes where not the kind to be heard in front his young student.

I had been in hospital for long over a month and was informed that my illness may have resulted in me not being able to have children. I was advised to take a test in a few years' time. The thought of perhaps not being able to have my own children depressed me as I dreamed of one day getting married and having lots of kids.

I was sent home for a week to regain my strength and then back to school. Once back at school I was told to rejoin the rugby team. During the first match I collided head on with a boy in the opposing team and cracked my forehead and was, once again "out of action". With that I missed almost a whole term at school.

Regrettably it had not been explained to me who was paying for my school fees, I assumed that it was my parents. I had heard discussions between my parents and their friends at home that it was not a good thing for taxpayers to finance others to go to private school. Then the subject came up during a discussion in class and not knowing any better I voiced the opinion, which was that of my parents. The teacher then informed me in front of the class that "Hallifax's fees where paid for by the Council". No, it was not something our teacher should have said in front of my class friends, and of course this I found to be deeply humiliating.

I loved my parents, but regrettably they found it hard to live in their financial reality, which is probably the reason for them not informing me of the Council paying for my school fees.

But never mind! Luckily for me music was again to come to my rescue.

On the 25th June 1967 we received permission to witness an historic event. I remember how excited I was as I sat in the school TV room to witness the world's first live-televised-satellite broadcast. Britain's contribution was "The Beatles" who performed their song *"All You Need is Love"*.

I had made up my mind to leave Eccles Hall School as soon as I was of the legal age to do so and that was at 16yrs. My parents and the school asked me the question, "what will you do Richard after leaving school?". "After all Richard you have no academic qualifications, and you have problems with reading and writing". They were trying very hard to persuade me to think again and continue at school. Pointing out that my chances of finding a job where extremely limited.

I never did tell my parents of the horrors that went on at Eccles Hall; if I had it would only have caused them to be ashamed, and I felt they had more than enough to cope with, given that Mother was not well, and that their personal finances were at rock bottom.

The school had invested in a careers cabinet full of leaflets providing information on various jobs and careers. The Vice Head Teacher suggested that "I take a look". I asked him if there was anything on how to become a male model, and he gave me a strange look. Another boy asked if there was anything on how to become a spy. The master who had ordered the cabinet could not believe it, as he had information on almost every other profession.

I decided to go into "show business", and after much thought I figured out that a way in could be through becoming a male model. Thanks to my parents, noticing an advertisement in a newspaper placed by The London Academy of Modeling, I found a path forward. Having applied, I was called to audition at the Academy's studios in New Bond Street in London. For this I would need time off from school and thankfully that was given. I accept that everyone who applied to the Academy was accepted; they just wanted the money, never-the-less for me this was a way forward into the world of "show business"!

The Academy taught me the technique of how to walk on a "catwalk", to pose as a photographic model, as well as how to work in front of television cameras. My course began on the 3rd April 1967 and lasted for three weeks. At the end of the course we students performed in front of friends and family in a live fashion show. My friend Chip and his sister Bets came together with my family to watch. I then returned to Eccles Hall.

It was the summer of 1967 and I was almost sixteen. For my school friends it was the summer holidays, but for me it was forever. As our bus departed from the school gates, I promised myself that I would never to return to that place.

Having lived the experience of being sent away to boarding school I am of the firm opinion that these institutions should not be allowed to exist. I am fully aware that there are many who disagree. Children should be at home with their families where they are surrounded with love and security. Yes, some families experience a lot of trouble, but home is surely a better place to be, rather than in an institution with strangers who do not provide any love whatsoever.

It is important to point out that Eccles Hall School is in no way to be confused with (The New Eccles Hall School) or (Aurora Eccles Hall School), both of which have fine reputations.

# Chapter 4

## There is No Business, like Show Business

Now that I had finally left school, I was looking forward to spending lots of time with my friend Chip. But that was not to happen, as sadly, Chip and his family had to return to the United States. At the same time my family had to move from the rented farmhouse that we all loved so much, this was because the owner wanted to sell and Mum and Dad where not in the financial position to purchase the house. The only consolation was when we heard who had bought the farmhouse – it was the then well-known actor Lionel Jeffries, perhaps best known for his role in the film "Chitty Chitty Bang Bang". At the time it was fun to say guess who moved into our old house!

Mum and Dad had no money whatsoever, so we moved to a rented counsel house in the village of Stoke Poges, which is located 2.7 miles north-east of Slough. Our new home was situated in an attractive area, but the house was too small for the six of us as there were only three small bedrooms. It must have been hard for my parents who had both been brought up under very different circumstances. Dad's father was managing director of a company in the Shell Oil group; his family had lived in large house with extensive grounds. My Grandfather had his own chauffer and employed people to run his house. Mother was also raised in a relatively wealthy home, her father an inventor, and her mother's family owned a hair-products firm. But now, due to circumstances beyond their control with Mum being unwell for so many years and Dad finding it hard to hold onto a job, things had changed, and it was hard for them to accept their new reality. So now that we were living in a council house Mum and Dad referred to it being "an upper income group council house", which it was, but it was still a council house. I suppose living in some kind of fantasy made it easier for them to accept their new situation.

Having finally found my freedom after leaving school I was looking forward to taking a long holiday before finding a job, and hopefully work in "show business" for real. But that was not going to happen, at least not yet. The pressure was on for me to contribute towards my food and lodgings at home and find a job, any job, and quick.

And that happened fast. My first job was in a sports shop in Windsor. The shop was owned by Stan Eldon the well-known British distance runner. As assistant to the shop manager my duties included scooping up live maggots and selling them to sports fisherman. I also sold running shoes and clothing. My weekly pay of seven pounds was just enough to cover my bus fair and to buy my egg and tomato sandwich for lunch. I saw little point in this as I had no money over for anything else, so after seven weeks I quit.

Thanks to Dad noticing an advertisement in the local paper, placed by the Daphne Webster model agency, I took my chance and called. Daphne wanted to meet me for an interview as soon as possible. I went to meet her at her home in Ascot. I took with me my portfolio of photos together with my certificate from the London Academy of Modeling. Daphne must have been impressed, because soon after our meeting engagements began to come in. My fee for an hour's work as a model was more than I made in a week at the sports shop, and I also got to be with some very beautiful young women. And when modeling at the live fashion shows the girls and I shared the same dressing room!

*Fun to be a mail model. Photo Slough Observer.*

I loved all the attention, being photographed, and all the kind compliments! People saying "you're good at this Richard" and "well done, your great", was quite the opposite to what I had been used to at school where all I heard was how terrible I was, "Richard you must improve", "you are last in the class", "it will be hard for you to find a job". But now, as a model, I was the center of attention.

The highlight of my first months in "show business" came when "The Beatles" had a hit in December 1967 with their song *"Hello Goodbye"*. I received a call from Daphne for a booking. "The Beatles" song was heading to the number one position on the BBC program "Top of the Pops". The Beatles had recorded a promo film for *"Hello Goodbye"*, but the film was not accepted by the BBC because in June 1966 the Musicians Union had secured a ban on all performances on television that were mimed. It was apparently obvious that The Beatles were miming on their film for the song. Therefore the BBC hastily arranged to make an alternative promotional film. I was one of four actors engaged to be in the production. We were filmed in a garden with clips of us appearing and disappearing in sync with the lyric *"Hello, Goodbye"*. As a point of interest at the time! this promotional film received more screenings on "Top of the Pops" than any of the official promotional films for the song.

As I was meeting with other actors and models my contact network widened, and I was introduced to several other agencies, one of which was Denton de Gray, based in London's West End on Great Windmill Street. I decided to pay them a visit.

Having walked past the strip clubs in London's Soho district I found the entrance to the office of Denton De Gray. Their office was on the second floor of the building, I walked up the stairs and into the reception. At one end of the room was a small opening covered with wire mesh, behind which was a small, sliding hatch, I noticed a door bell, which I pressed, the bell rang and when the hatch opened a young woman asked "and what can I do for you sir, are you looking for work?". "Yes" I replied, and after providing her with information regarding my experience I was shown through to meet Mr. Denton De Gray, a legend in the world of British show business. Mr. De Gray liked me, and I heard later that he was especially impressed with my good manners! "My boarding school had given my something", I thought. Then I was introduced to Lena. Lena oversaw bookings. Luckily, Lena also liked me. A few days later my phone rang, and engagements came flooding in. First, I was booked as a walk-on artist, and later for speaking parts on TV programs. I appeared on many popular shows including the BBC TV production: "The first night of Pygmalion", a BBC TV production "Dance of the seven veils", directed by Ken Russell, "The Benny Hill Show" and a "Cliff Richard" Christmas special for ATV Television. I also did some stunt work and was engaged to "double" for Jamie in the "Dr Who" series, "The Enemy of the World" and "The Mind Robber".

In many ways working in films and television is just the same as in any other job, at least when it comes to working hours. I would have to sometimes get myself up as early as five am in order to catch the train from Gerrards Cross railway station, and then the tube from Ruislip Station to Shepherds Bush in London, in order to get to the BBC Television Center on time to start work. On occasion a coach would then transport us actors and artists to locations for filming in and around the London area. I recall one of these coach trips in particular, whereupon I received some very sound advice. I was sitting next to a colleague who had been in Show Business for many years. He said to me that in Show Business one would sometimes be in the front of the bus, and sometimes in the back. But the trick was to make sure that one always remained on the bus!

It was important to promote myself, so I advertised myself in the "Spotlight" casting directory from August the 19th 1970 to February 1971 under the section: Actors. A casting director employed by a TV company noticed my photo and called me. He said that he may have a part for me in a TV series and that he wanted me to come to his office in London for an interview. I couldn't believe my luck and went to meet him. During the interview he led me to believe that I had a real chance of getting the part, but that he wanted me to visit him at his home and take some photos of me. Being young and naïve I agreed. When I arrived at his flat, he suggested that we go outside to take some photos because it would be good to have the natural daylight, he explained. Having taken photos of me outside he suggested we go into his flat and take some more. Thinking nothing of it I agreed, however, once we were inside he asked me to undress as he wanted to take photos of me naked. Not again I thought! One of the main reasons I had decided to leave school at such a young age was to get away from immoral people, but here I was, now face-to-face with yet another person who clearly had the intent of abusing me. This person had no intention of offering me a part in a TV production. He was "grooming" me. I left, but the danger for me now was that I was beginning to think that this sort of behavior was normal.

I am not blaming anyone, but the damage done to my psychology was going to take most of my life to heal, I will go further, the immorality I came face to face with as a young person at school and in show business almost ruined my life. It is regrettable that from a young age I was not given any sexual education. Had I received such an education and been told that there where people such as pedophiles, I would have been wiser to their predatory nature and had a chance to avoid them. Also, I would have been far better equipped to cope with life if I had understood how my body would naturally change at puberty, but things were as they were and I was learning the hard way, and sadly, at times, the wrong way. I will also add the immorality I came face-to-face with at school, and in show business, resulted in a silent "mental unhappiness" throughout most of my adult life. It is only thanks to my faith in God that I have managed to remain somewhat balanced.

But there were genuine, professional photographers, whom I worked with in the modeling and show business world for advertising campaigns. One of which was for "Interflora", the flower-delivery network. In this campaign my face was on posters in every tube station throughout London. It was fun noticing people taking a second look at me as I walked past the posters when travelling on London's underground system. Once again, I felt that I was in "the center" and a "somebody".

# Chapter 5

## First Love

"*The First Cut is The Deepest*" is a song written by "Cat Stevens", and reflects the emotion most of us feel when our first experience of "falling in love" comes to an end.

During the summer of 1968 the family took a holiday. We were loaned my Grandmother's (Grannies) caravan, which was permanently parked on a caravan site at Bognor Regis, located on the south coast of England in the county of West Sussex.

Dad parked his car next to Grannies caravan making it easier for the family to unpack. Whist unloading our bags I glanced over to the other side of the caravan site and noticed a very attractive girl who was together with her family. She had a "French look" about her, which I found attractive. Her long, light-brown, wavy hair, fluttered slightly in the warm breeze, and as she moved her body I thought she looked like a Russian, Olympic gymnast. I could not take my eyes off her. The two adults must be her parents and the younger girl her sister I thought; they were doing the same as us, taking their bags from their car and into their caravan, so they must be here to stay, I hoped. I decided to walk over and introduce myself.

"Hi, my name is Richard, how long are you planning on staying?" I asked, and to my delight the mother in the family replied that they would be staying for a few weeks. Looking at the girl who had caught my eye I asked, "and what is your name?" She looked directly into my eyes and replied, "My name is Margaret". I felt as though I had been hypnotized! For the first time in my life I had instantly and completely "fallen in love". Thoughts flashed through my head, this is the girl I am going to marry and have children with. Margaret and I are going to spend the rest of our lives together and one day we shall marry. I felt a complete feeling of happiness throughout my whole being.

I found it hard to sleep as I wondered how I was going to make my next move. I decided that I would invite Margaret to go for a walk with me. As soon as I was up, and having plucked up enough courage, I went over to Margaret's caravan and knocked on the door to invite her to join me. "I will have to ask my parents" she replied, followed by "yes, I would love to if it is ok with them". At first Margaret's parents were not too keen on the two of us walking alone, after all we had only just met, and "Margaret was not yet 16 yrs old", her mother said, but if we could walk with others it would be ok. I quickly spread the word, first asking my brothers and sister, and then other young people we knew on the caravan site if they would accompany us for a walk. Most said yes and it wasn't long before there was a group of young people who had nothing better to do other than join us.

It was a beautiful, warm, summer's day, not a cloud in the sky. At first, we walked through fields filled with the scents of wild, summer flowers, and then on we went along winding, country lanes towards the sea. We heard the waves caressing the shoreline and smelt the freshness of the sea air as we approached the beach. Margaret and I talked a little and romantically looked at one another as we walked; then, slowly, we moved closer to one another with our hands almost touching. When we arrived at the beach, and without saying a word to one another, we separated ourselves from the others in the group ending up more or less on our own, with our hands moving from a delicate touch into holding and, maintaining eye contact, and without saying a word we had our first kiss.

The days passed and as Margaret's family got to know me, we were permitted to walk alone.

Time flew by and it wasn't long before our holiday came to an end. Margaret's mother, not wanting to separate us, kindly invited me to follow the family home to Brighton where they lived; I was welcome to stay for a week or two her mother said. I could not imagine being separated from Margaret and accepted the invitation immediately.

The following two weeks in Brighton passed in a flash, and then it was time for Margaret to go back to school and for me to return home.

During the autumn months that followed I must have driven my family mad, all I talked about was Margaret. My sister Nicola remembers to this day my repeating over and over "I love Margaret", "I want to be with Margaret", "I cannot live without Margaret".

I continued to work on various TV programs and had to make many trips to London. Christmas was approaching; and I wanted to buy Margaret a present. I gave a lot of thought as to what my gift should be. Finding it hard to decide I looked in the display windows of various shops in Oxford Street for inspiration. I was searching for something romantic, and eventually came up with what I thought would be the ideal gift.

I wanted to take our relationship to the next level, so I decided to buy her a very sexy, underwear kit. Having done so, I then decided to pack the frilly, red bra and panties, in multiple layers of paper so that my small gift would take on the appearance of being a very large packet. It would be more fun for her when opening my gift, I thought, as with every layer of paper the mystery of what lies inside would prolong the excitement. Stupidly I gave no thought to the possibility that Margaret might unpack her gift in front of her parents. Love is blind. I can only imagine the look on her parents faces when the very sexy underwear appeared. From that moment on I was of course no longer the wonderful boy their daughter had met!

After Christmas I could no longer stand being apart from Margaret. One evening after finishing work on a TV program, I decided to hop on the late train from Victoria train station in

London to Brighton. I was going to surprise Margaret and just turn up, I hoped that I would arrive late evening, but my journey took much longer than expected, I did not arrive until two am in the morning and of course at that time Margaret and her family where all sound asleep.

I decided to throw stones at Margaret's bedroom window and try to wake her, Romeo and Juliet I thought! Nothing happened so I kept trying, and still nothing, so in the end I rang the front doorbell and awoke the whole family, they were of course furious with the exception of Margaret who was delighted to see me!

With my shocking Christmas present and now waking the whole family in the middle of the night, Margaret's parents understandably had now had enough of me and did everything they could to end our relationship. "I was not to disrupt Margaret's studies" they said, and a meeting was arranged for both of our fathers to meet to discuss the situation. Our parents decided to interfere and suggested that we needed a "cooling off" period. From then on it became difficult for Margaret and me to meet. It is not easy to have a relationship when one's own family is not in support, and being apart from Margaret became unbearable for me. It would be easier to cope with the situation if I ended our relationship I decided. Not logical you may think, given that I was madly in love with her. But when emotions take over one does not think logically. So, I called Margaret to tell her that it was over, even though this was totally opposite to what my heart desired.

A couple of years passed and still the only girl I really wanted to be with was Margaret. I decided to call her on the phone, to my delight she wanted to meet me, but I have never fully understood why as she was now living with another guy. We decided that I would collect her and that we would go for a drive. She got into my car and we began to chat. Having caught up on what we had both been doing over the past two years the conversation became tense, I was not happy that she was with someone else, in fact I was jealous. And on reflection I said all the wrong things and it became clear that now our relationship really was over. But it hurt, it really hurt – *"The first cut is the deepest"*.

# Chapter 6

## With the Stars

Luckily for me I was working in "Show Business" and that provided me with opportunities to have lots of fun. For example, it was a real kick for me to be meeting celebrities such as "The Bee Gees", "Status Quo", John and Yoko, "Cliff Richard", "Lulu", Jimi Hendrix, in fact almost all the main pop stars of the time.

In 1971 "The Rolling Stones" arrived at the BBC Television Center to video a performance of their new song *"Brown Sugar"* for "Top of the Pops". The studio was cleared of all people, those remaining where the camera men, sound technicians, and the floor manager, and me. I took a chance and remained in the studio; luckily no one questioned my being there. This was probably because I was in and around "Top of the Pops" so often that I was almost a part of the scenery. So, I got to stay even though I was not essential crew.

It was Denton De Gray who asked me if I would like to work as a stand in on "Top of the Pops". And I embraced the opportunity. The program was sent out live, once a week, from the BBC studios in the Sheppard's Bush area of London. The first programs that I was involved in where broadcast from the BBC studios at Lime Grove, and later the Television Center at White City. "Top of the Pops" had an audience of at around 15 million people. All pop stars of the time wanted to appear on the program. During the day artists rehearsed together with the camera and sound crew, but did not always arrive on time, so stand-in's where needed. To be a stand in was part of my job, the other part was making sure that none of the dancing public got hurt when the cameras swung around suddenly and moved back and forth, which was necessary in order to get the best and most exciting TV shots of the artists as they performed.

One time during rehearsals I stood in for Keith Moon, who was the drummer in "The Who" rock band, apparently I did such a convincing performance that during the coffee break I was asked by someone who had been watching the monitor screens if I was Keith. On another occasion "Cat Stevens" was on the show. He had arrived in time for rehearsals, but his drummer was late so I stood in, even though I was miming I played the drums for real, Cat turned to me and said "pretty good", and I cheekily replied "need a drummer?", Cat looked directly at me as though I had over stepped the mark. On occasion I was, perhaps, "overconfident". Also, I recall in 1968 when "The Hollies" were at the BBC TV Lime Grove Studio, I overheard a conversation between Graham Nash, who was a member of "The Hollies" pop group, and one of the "Top of The Pops" presenters Jimmy Savile. Graham Nash was telling Jimmy that he was going to leave the Hollies and join up with David Crosby and Stephen Stills. Looking back on hearing their conversation and then seeing the success he had with his new group "Crosby Stills & Nash" was a cool conversation to have overheard.

So here I was having lots of fun and enjoying the privilege of working at BBC TV on Britain's top pop music program of the time "Top of The Pops" .To give you some Idea and sense of the fun I experienced whilst working on the show here are some more of my memories.

One day during 1968, as I looked down from a window at the BBC Lime Grove studio, I was excited to see the singer Tom Jones get out of the black London taxi cab that had brought him to the studio. Tom had arrived to perform his hit *Delilah*. Then I turned and noticed something that gave me even more of a buzz. Steve Marriott, lead singer and guitarist in the group "Small Faces" had cheekily driven his mini car into the service lift on the ground floor and then directly into the Top of the Pops studio! Those in charge where furious so he quickly took his car back down in the lift, I loved it. Steve was a pop star and he could do whatever he liked; he must have thought. Then I was in the cafeteria at the back of the studio sitting together with the groups "The Bee Gees" and "Status Quo", both experiencing their first hits in the pop charts. "The Bee Gees" with the song *Massachusetts* and "Status Quo" with the song *Pictures of Matchstick Men*. I was a young, sixteen-year-old, so for me the experience of being there with these pop stars was more than exciting. Being involved with "Top of the Pops" was something that my friends and most young people could only dream of at the time.

Everything was great until one day whilst passing a dressing room a man stopped me and invited me in. In the room were several men who were watching a pornographic film. Having had no sexual education, I was curious and took a look. Aside from being shocked I now knew what sex was all about, well that is what I thought at the time, because it was in hindsight a bad way to learn. On the other hand, it made me sick to my stomach to know that some people who were working on Britain's top pop-music program had no sense of morality. My thoughts flashed back to my time at school and the immoral teachers who I had escaped from. Obviously, the authorities at BBC TV knew nothing of this. Had it been known that people working for the Corporation and especially on "Top of the Pops" – a program for young people, had been watching such a film in a dressing room at the studio, the program's reputation could have been ruined.

"Top of the Pops" had four main presenters during the period 1967-1969. They were Jimmy Savile, Pete Murray, Alan Freeman and Tony Blackburn. I said "hi" to all four of them on a regular basis, and on occasion had a chat. At the time all four men seemed to be very pleasant people. I looked up to them; after all they were "star" Disc Jockeys (DJ's) and national celebrities, almost to the same level as some of the pop and rock bands.

Since the age of fifteen I had been writing songs and decided to seek some help and advice on how to make contact with a recording company, and, or, a music publisher. Considering that I was surrounded by people connected to the music business I took a chance and mentioned this to the presenter Alan Freeman. Alan invited me to visit him at his home in Maida Vale in London. I couldn't wait to play him my songs hoping that he would help me. My parents warned me to be careful, in case he may be interested in me for other reasons, because there was a rumor that he was attracted to the male sex.

I took the train from Gerrards Cross to Marylebone station in London and then found my way to Alan's flat in Maida Vale. I was overwhelmed when I entered his penthouse apartment. It was luxurious, with a huge window reaching up over two floors. On the first floor was an expensive-looking suite of chairs and a grand piano that stood under a spiral stairway which led up to a bedroom on a balcony, from where one could look down to the sitting-room area. Through the sitting room was an office where photos of pop stars together with Alan where displayed on a wall. I was very impressed with one photo in particular. It was of Alan together with Paul McCartney, and the photo had been taken in the apartment. I was with someone who not only knew a Beatle, but had been his guest in this same apartment. For me as a young, teenage boy, this was very impressive. Outside was a large roof garden with a set of chairs and a television. Alan made a very nice meal for the two of us and then listened to my songs. It soon became clear that Alan *was* attracted to me. Sadly, by now, I was quite used to men making advances to me, but I made it clear to him that I was not gay, which he respected and over time we became good friends. Alan loved my song "*Mr. Man in the Moon*" and introduced me to the music publishers Carlin Music, who later signed a contract with me for some of my songs.

I had written "*Mr. Man in the Moon*" after my friend Chip had returned to the U.S. Chip had a sister and I fantasized about falling in love with her, marring her, and going to the U.S. to live happily ever after together with Chip and his family. So, the words of the song are about the "Man in the Moon borrowing his broom and sweeping the sea away", so that I could walk over to the U.S. This seemed a good idea as I could not afford the air or boat ticket at the time. Anyway, it was all just a dream that I turned into a song.

Besides being a presenter on "Top of The Pops", Alan also had his own radio program on "208 Radio Luxemburg," – "the station of the stars", which was broadcast to listeners all over Europe. The station had a small recording studio at No 38 Hertford Street in London, which was primarily used for pre-recording radio programs that were later broadcasted from the country of Luxemburg. I went with Alan to watch him record one of his radio shows, whilst there I found out that it was possible to hire the studio for private use. This I did and a few days later when I returned to the studio to record some of my music, which I then had pressed on to an Acetate disc (a type of gramophone record), with my songs on record I could present my music to the publishing and recording companies in the hope that they might be interested in signing me.

On the 11th of February 1970, John Lennon and Yoko Ono arrived at the BBC "Top of the Pops" studio to perform their hit song *Instant Karma*. At the time John was not my favorite Beatle, I had not liked his comment in 1966 when he said words to the effect of "that the public was more infatuated with the Beatles than with Jesus", and I wasn't keen on Yoko either. I had got it into my head that she was responsible for splitting up the Beatles, of course I had no idea if that was true or not, it was probably something I had read in a newspaper. In any case I took the opportunity to introduce myself to them and to my surprise they both came across to me as very nice people, in fact I completely changed my mind about both of them, they gave me their time and listened to what I had to say. I asked John if he would be kind enough to pass my demonstration record on to someone at Apple Records, and he said he would. Later, after the recording for the program (to be broadcast on the 12th) I met them again when they were leaving and gave them my Demo. John asked if my contact details where written on the record cover, and I checked. On the demo was a song I had written together with my band at Eccles Hall School. The song title was *"Free as a Bird"*. I never heard again from John or Apple Records. But On the 4th December 1995 the Beatles released *"Free as a Bird"* – a song written by John Lennon in 1977. I have always wondered if John did listen to my demo and perhaps was inspired, probably not, but then again who knows!

I found it surprising and refreshing how down to earth the celebrities I met where in person. Cliff Richard was my first pop idol. I never imagined in my wildest dreams that I would ever get to meet him. But I did, and I would like to share the experience with you. Whilst working with Cliff on his Christmas television program for ATV in December 1968 we got chatting during rehearsals, during the conversation I asked Cliff if he kept a scrap book with newspaper cuttings about his career, to which he replied yes. The next day, much to my surprise, he brought his scrap book with him to show me. We sat together on the stairs leading into the rehearsal hall and he spent time going through his scrap book and telling me all about his experiences. On another occasion, whilst at my music publishers Carlin Music I met Cliff coming down the stairs carrying a mattress over his shoulder. The mattress had been used to help with acoustics whilst recording one of his songs. Cliff had been kind enough to help a woman carry the mattress to her car. Nice guy I thought, showing that we never know what someone is like. After Jimmy Savile passed away on the 29 October 2011, hundreds of allegations of sexual abuse were made against him. This came as a complete surprise to me even though it was known that Jimmy *liked* girls. As I have already stated, I had often said "hello" to Jimmy at

"Top of the Pops" and he always seemed pleasant. Although I never knew him privately Jimmy always gave the impression that he was "Mr. nice guy". But yes, from my own experience, and as we have learnt, there were a few people associated with the program who abused the power of their position. But that does not mean the program was bad. "Top of the Pops" was a fantastic TV program enjoyed by millions of people, and in my view one of the best programs ever produced by the BBC. Even though I played a very small role in the production of the program, I am very proud to have been part of its history.

# Chapter 7

## *The Opportunity of a Lifetime*

There are events that happen during one's lifetime that must be mentioned. One of those happened on July 20 1969 when the world watched Neal Armstrong take his first steps on the Moon. This was a dream come true for most of us, and has inspired me ever since to hold on to the belief that all things are possible.

But, whilst that was a great step for mankind, on Earth, at home, things weren't so good. Dad did not have a job and was living on unemployment pay. I was still drawing in an income from my work on various TV programs and that continued until around 1972, however there weren't enough engagements coming in for me to live off the income. Dad and I spent most days watching TV at home. My Mother on the other hand, who had not been well for years, suddenly, to everyone's surprise went out and got a job driving cleaning women to and from their place of work. This was an incredible decision for my mother to have made and showed great courage given what she had been through.

Word got around that Dad and I needed work. Upon hearing, a friend of the family with his own business presented us with the opportunity of a lifetime. At least that was the sales pitch. An American cosmetics company built upon pyramid selling was setting up in the UK. If you had a little bit of start-up capital, you could buy your way in to the different levels of the pyramid-structured scheme. For example, direct door-to-door sales for a small investment, or with a larger investment you could become a supplier, higher up in the chain. Having very little else to do, Dad and I decided to give it a try. But there was just one small problem, we had no capital.

Fortunately, our friend had already bought into the "Holiday Magic" business plan and was only too pleased to give us a loan. We needed one thousand pounds to get started – quite a lot of money in those days. With the loan we bought stock from him which increased his sales so that he qualified for a higher place in the pyramid, providing him with a larger pay packet. Dad and I established a sales team, mostly young friends of mine who were only too pleased to get hold of some extra cash, and we began to sell cosmetics.

Then in my spare time, together with my cousin Malcolm, we built a mobile discotheque and sound system made from old turn tables from our parents' gramophones, together with a homemade mixer board and some old loudspeakers donated by a friend. The next step was to have some records to play. As they were expensive for us to buy, I called my DJ friend Alan Freeman in the hope that he had records that we could have for free. Alan was only too pleased to help. I travelled to Maida Vale in west London where Alan lived and he kindly gave us a large bag full of 45 rpm singles, many of them promotional records, all very impressive for us young DJ's as the records had the letter "A" printed on one side. This was done so that DJ's would play the potential hit side of the record. Then, thanks to "Holiday Magic" we got some bookings and supplied background music at their various events. Needing a name for our venture we decided to call our discotheque business "Audio Two Sound Services". I had no idea at the time that this experience was a rehearsal for much bigger things to come.

*"Audio Two" me on the left and my cousin Malcolm. Photo private.*

Because of our great team of sales' girls selling door-to-door it did not take long before we had sold our initial stock of "Holiday Magic" cosmetics. We were able to pay back the loan of one thousand pounds in full. Dad and I decided to carry on with our business project but without "Holiday Magic".

We set up a company and named it "Circle Marketing International Sales Ltd". With the initial success of selling cosmetics we were now back on our feet. Dad, with his experience in sales and marketing, set about finding new products for us to sell. He approached consulates from several countries. At the Norwegian consulate a Mr. Kristiansen was looking for a company in England that could sell electric radiators that where manufactured in Norway. Because Dad was born in Sweden, his Scandinavian roots helped in developing a good relationship with Mr. Kristiansen and we succeeded in securing a contract to import the radiators. Mr. Kristiansen put us in touch with a firm in London called Warm Heat; they were interested in selling the radiators from Norway. After meeting Warm Heat, we had our first customer. There was, however, a catch to this, not seen by us at the time. Warm Heat was not credit worthy in the eyes of the Norwegian bank, but our firm Circle Marketing was. In order to import the heaters Dad and I would be required to sign credit notes. This was necessary so that the bank in Norway would continue to finance the radiator factory in Norway. The plan could work providing the Norwegians could wait for 90 days for payment and that our customers paid us on time.

It did not take long before we found other customers who wanted to buy electric radiators. Business was so good that within a short time we were able to afford to move the office out of the house and into an office building.

After some searching, we found suitable offices in the town of High Wycombe, which is situated about 30 miles North West of London. Our offices were on the top floor of the two-story building at Totteridge Avenue, and consisted of four large rooms and one small. One office room for me, and one for Dad, later we employed two salesmen and a secretary who worked in the other rooms. Dad and I bought a car each, for Dad a Jaguar XJ6 and for me a Ford Cortina. Then we increased our product range, which included importing sailing yachts from Norway. It was important for us to visit our Norwegian suppliers, so Dad and I made several visits to the country. On these trips I fell in love with Norway and its beautiful nature.

I was responsible for what became our marine division and

arranged to show our company products at various exhibitions. During one such exhibition, at a boat show at Little Venice in London, I decided to look around and see what the other companies were exhibiting. As I made my way around, I could not help but notice a very attractive, young woman. She was so beautiful that she caught my full attention. I felt drawn to her like a magnet to metal; I must introduce myself I thought. "Hello, my name is Richard, what do you think of little Venice", I asked politely. "Oh, I love it, such a beautiful place with the boats on the canal and the cafes", she replied. We continued our conversation and having established that we were both single I asked Irena if she would like to meet me again. I will think about it she replied. I explained why I was at the exhibition and pointed to the sailing yacht in the canal that belonged to my company hoping that she would be impressed, and I said that if she wished I would be happy to show her the boat, perhaps tomorrow I suggested. The next day came so I went over to Irena and asked again, "yes I would love to take a look" she said, we walked together to the boat and I invited Irena to come on board. And that is how our relationship began.

Irena knew a couple who were from Canada, Larry and Marie. Larry worked in Maidenhead by the river Thames, he also sold boats. Occasionally the couple invited us over for dinner and sometimes we stayed overnight. Larry and Marie smoked joints and explained to Irena and me that in Canada most of the people they knew smoked joints. In any event smoking joints was not for me. However, during one of our visits, my curiosity got the better of me, so I gave it a go. I puffed and I puffed, only to experience nothing. Perhaps I was using the wrong technique, but smoking their joints was, for me, just the same as smoking a cigarette.

Irena was of Polish decent and being Catholic we shared the same faith. We became very fond of one another and decided to get engaged.

On the business side of my life, Circle Marketing was going so well that Dad and I had enough money to buy a 34ft ocean, sailing yacht which we named Desert Island. We sailed to France, the Channel Islands, and one summer down the west coast of England. On the 11th August 1971 we sailed into Plymouth harbor. Having moored at the visitors mooring, the harbor master asked us to move our boat, explaining that we had to make space for "Morning Cloud" – the racing yacht owned by the then British Prime Minister, Edward Heath. We ended up moving to a mooring about 30ft from where we were and watched, at close quarters, the arrival of Edward Heath at the helm of "Morning Cloud". There was great excitement because we were so close to a very important person and thousands of people were gathered on the quayside looking down towards the Prime Minister and us.

Whilst working with the marine products division of Circle Marketing I decided to begin a new project to work with on the side. Using my experience from my modeling days I decided to start a model agency which I named "Personality Girl". I had kept in touch with some of the girls I had worked with from the time when I had been a model. My modeling friends were delighted as I managed to arrange quite a few jobs for them. I recall one company, who manufactured bras, calling and asking for models, I then had to phone my girls and ask them what size cup do you have? Most embarrassing!

During this time, I remembered the advice I had received from when I was in hospital in Norwich with my swollen testicles. I decided it was time to take a test so that I would know as to whether I was fertile or not. I had already accepted that perhaps I was not. When the results came back, I was overjoyed to know that all was well.

Keen to keep trying with my song writing I established a partnership with a friend also named Richard. He worked as a sound engineer at De Lane Lea Studios in London. Richard was able to use the studio for free when no one else was recording. This provided an opportunity for us to record songs I had written. Late one evening whilst recording, Richard buzzed me from the control room and said we had to leave because the studio had been hired out to someone. I noticed a man coming down the steps into the sound studio with a guitar. He left his guitar and had said "hi" to me. I was behind the sound screen playing my guitar and did not pay too much attention as to who he was. Upon joining Richard in the control room, he asked me if I had seen who it was. He went on to say that it was Paul McCartney. I wish to this day that we had remained at the studio, but Richard's boss wanted us out.

As a point of interest The Beatles, The Rolling Stones, Bee Gees, The Who, The Jimi Hendrix Experience, and Pink Floyd are just some of the groups who have recorded songs in the studios, and me!

# Chapter 8

## The Coal-Miners' Strike

As my Grand Mother always said, "in life there is always a something".

In 1974 the Coal Miners in the UK were on strike again! And this led to frequent power cuts, and that led to a three-day working week for the whole country. The market for electric heaters came to a grinding halt almost overnight. Our main customers were unable to pay their bills, which meant that we had no income and could not pay our bills to the factory in Norway. This resulted in the Norwegian factory not being able to manufacture electric heaters. It did not take long before our business, Circle Marketing International Sales Ltd, was forced into liquidation. I had to sell almost everything I owned and leave the house I was renting with three friends, because I no longer had an income I was unable to pay my share of the rent.

The house that I and my three friends rented was situated on Scotland's Drive in Farnham Common, Bucks, which is about three miles north of Slough. I shared a room with my friend Angus; our other two, house mates, Phil and Martin, paid a little more rent than Angus and me because they had their own bedrooms. We took it in turns to do the shopping, cooking, and cleaning; this was all good experience for us regarding the domestic side of life. Best of all we had lots of parties. I was sorry that I had to leave. I have many fond memories from my time together with my three friends, but there is one memory in particular, that sticks out. It was an autumn night, Angus and I had gone to bed, and we had left our bedroom window open to allow for some extra air to come into the room. Autumn leaves had fallen and covered the long lawn that ended at a fence where there was a public foot path on the other side. Half asleep I heard a sound, as if somebody had hopped over the fence, then the rustling of leaves and footsteps – someone was walking towards our bedroom window, I woke Angus. He quietly picked up a heavy microphone stand which I had in our room and stood behind the window curtain poised to hit the person over the head when he came through the window. I was convinced that this might kill the fellow, so I quietly woke the others, Martin and Phil. Once up they opened the back door, ran out and chased the person to one side of the house where there was an old, rusty car. The person jumped onto the roof of the car and disappeared over a fence which separated the front garden from the back garden, and our house from the neighbours. Martin and Phil, thinking that the intruder was now at the front side of our house, circled in opposite directions, meeting in the front, both thinking that the other was the intruder. Then, as they were about to throw a punch at each other, with fists clenched and arms raised, they realized who was who! The intruder was never seen again.

My roommate Angus had a girlfriend who was dating Paul Grade, the son of Lord Lew Grade. Lord Grade was a business tycoon who founded ATV Television, ITC Films, and ATV Music. ATV at that time owned "The Beatles" catalog of songs. I was introduced to Paul; we kept in touch and in the years that followed we become very good friends.

Having to give up my room and leave my friends was only one of the consequences of the liquidation of Circle Marketing; it also burdened me with a lot of financial stress and worry. This influenced everything, including my private life. My fiancé Irena gave me all the support she could, in fact she was fantastic. But I was deeply depressed, and I found it hard to sleep or think straight. I was not myself; I became selfish and worried a lot about my future. Having a serious relationship or considering marriage was, at the time, just another "burden" to carry. So, I ended my relationship with Irena.

Looking back, I can now understand why things had not worked out as I had thought they would. At the time when everything seemed to be going wrong, it was in fact going right! God had other plans for me. If I had trusted God as I do now, I would have found it much easier to handle the crises I was in.

I sold one of my two last remaining assets, my stereo, and with the money I paid for a trip to Norway. My other asset was my guitar, which I decided not to sell. I thought if all else fails I could always earn some money by playing the guitar and singing my songs.

I had a girlfriend living in Oslo who had invited me to stay. I had been introduced to Anna by my best friend Robert, who also had a Norwegian girlfriend. After being introduced to Anna I had kept in touch with her. Now, you are probably thinking – "you bastard!", you were engaged to Irena and you have another girl in Norway. Well that is true; however, up to now my relationship with Anna had been purely platonic.

Needing a new start, a holiday, and a chance to get away from all the problems to do with our failed business, the opportunity to stay with Anna in Oslo seemed to be a good idea. Besides, Anna lived with her mother so there was little chance of anything happening between us, we were just friends.

I travelled from London to Oslo by train, first to Harwich then by ferry to the Hook of Holland and then up through Germany, Denmark, Sweden, to Norway.

As the train passed through Gothenburg in Sweden I looked out of the window and thought that the place looked very industrial and that I would never want to choose to live there. After my long journey the train arrived at Oslo Central Station and there to meet me was Anna.

I was delighted to be back in Oslo. Here, I felt more at home than in England. Perhaps it was because my father was born in

Stockholm and had spoken so fondly of Scandinavia, or maybe it was because of my previous visits to the country. Anna had borrowed her mother's car and drove me to their small apartment where there were only two bedrooms, so I slept in the lounge on a sofa. Their apartment was on the second floor and had a small balcony. I loved looking out and seeing the tall, pine trees. That summer in 1974 the weather in Oslo was fabulous, during my three-month stay the sun shone every single day.

Before I was to return to England, I decided to visit Stockholm wanting to see where Dad had been brought up. I travelled by train from Oslo with my guitar and very little money. In fact, I had to find work to earn enough money for my trip back. On arrival to Stockholm I could not help but notice the students who were wearing white caps, shouting, singing and drinking. I was told they were celebrating leaving collage (graduating). Not knowing where to go or what to do, I found a taxi and asked the driver for advice. He told me to hop into his cab and kindly drove me to a youth hostel, which was on a boat moored at "Söder Mälarstrand". There he left me. It was late, around eleven pm. With no one to be seen I went onboard the boat and having no choice I slept under the cover that protected the entrance to the cabin door. I did not sleep well because during the summer months in Sweden there is almost twenty-four-hour daylight. In a way the light was good because I am afraid of the dark! And luckily because it was summer, the outdoor temperature was warm. In the morning the owner arrived and provided me with a cabin which I was to share with whoever else turned up. I explained that I had no money to pay him with, but that I had my guitar and could sing. Needing entertainment in his restaurant he engaged me to perform. The owner also paid me to paint the deck of another boat he owned. So, it wasn't long before I had enough money for my return trip to Oslo. During my stay in Stockholm a main event took place on the 15th of June 1974 when Princess Christina, sister of the Swedish King (Carl XVI

Gustaf), married Tord Magnusson. I enjoyed watching some of the celebrations from the boat. Then, before taking the train back to Oslo I went to see the house where my father had been brought up in Saltsjöbaden, which lies approximately nine English miles south of Stockholm.

I returned to Oslo for a few days before returning to England. It was hard leaving Anna, because after our time together I was beginning to fall in love with her. But that's life; my travel visa had run out, so I had to leave the country.

I felt depressed upon my arrival back in England. Having nowhere to live I had little choice but to moved back in with Mum and Dad. But where was I going to sleep? My brother Charles had inherited my bedroom after I had moved out. Thankfully he was kind enough to share his room with me. But I had to sleep on a mattress on the floor. This was because there was not a spare bed, and no one in the family could afford to buy one.

My first priority was to find a job. Through a London job agency I was recommended to a company who were the agents for "Rukka" rainwear products, which the firm imported from Finland.

The company office and warehouse were located on the other side of Heathrow Airport, not too far from where we lived; however, it took ages to drive there in all the traffic. The boss was a woman who was impressed with my experience from Circle Marketing as well as my knowledge of Scandinavia, and I also felt that maybe she fancied me! Without hesitation she offered me the job. This meant I would be travelling to shops all over London to sell "Rukka" rainwear. I was three weeks into the job when I made a terrible mistake. I had gone to visit a shop at a yacht marina on the river Thames in London and met a very famous female sailor, whom I shall not name. As I had an interest in sailing it was easy to start a conversation with her, she told me that her main work was in marketing so I thought she would be a good contact for my new boss. I also found her attractive and asked if she would like to come out for a date sometime. This got back to my boss. I have no idea of what was said but my boss made it clear that she did not like that I had asked the famous sailor for a date. I was told that my services where no longer required. I was given a cheque for 300 pounds and that was that.

Having gone through all the problems with the collapse of Circle Marketing this was the last thing I needed. I was rock bottom and it did go through my mind to contemplate suicide. What is the point in living if everything and everyone is against me, I thought. At that moment I could not see a way forward with my life. There I was with no job, no income, and no hope; I thought that I was a complete failure, having now lost my new job, what would people think of me?

Having read up about suicide it is interesting to note that two of the many causes of people wanting to take their own lives are sexual abuse and unemployment.

I called my DJ friend Alan Freeman and hearing how I sounded he suggested that I come straight over and visit him. As I travelled across London on the tube train, I was in such a state that my body shivered, and I could not stop the tears as they rolled down the cheeks of my face.

Upon seeing the state I was in, Alan did everything he could to calm me down. He began by telling me that I had a lot of living to do and that I was not to give up. He advised me to put the three hundred pounds in the bank and look for another job. You will have to pay your bills next month, the month after that, then the year after that he said. Now, you may be thinking that this was the last thing I needed to hear, but his words had quite the opposite effect. Alan was giving me a reality check and it did me good to be lectured on life's realities and responsibilities. After our long chat I returned home.

Sadly, I have known two people who have taken their own lives, one a great friend of mine and the other a relative of my wife. If you yourself, or if you know someone who has such thoughts, please do not hesitate to seek immediate, expert help.

But as things turned out it wasn't long before I found work as an assistant gardener at a pharmaceutical company near to where my family and I lived in Stoke Poges. One of my duties was to cut the grass. The company had its own private pub, so I enjoyed drinking a pint of beer at lunch time, after which it was not so easy to cut the grass in straight lines. Which is very important when cutting grass in England! Although I enjoyed gardening the pay was not too good, so I found a better paying job at the ICI paint factory in Slough. This was to be my first experience at working on a production line. Sometimes the automated line moved so fast that we, human workers, couldn't keep up with the manual loading of the paint cans. So, when we needed an extra break one of us working on the line intentionally knocked over a can of paint. This stopped production for a while and gave us a much-needed breathing space. Finding the work totally unstimulating I could not see myself staying in the factory for long.

# Chapter 9

## International Disc Jockey

The year was 1975; I was now 24 years old. Whilst on one of my regular visits to the local pub, I began to chat with a man who was sitting at the bar. We discussed jobs; he told me that he was going to audition for DJ work in London. I asked him if he would give me the telephone number of the people he was going to see, and he did.

The next day I called the number he had given me. It didn't take long before I was on my way to the office of London Town Discotheques, which was located at Blenheim Street, not far from New Bond Street. I took with me my references and photos from my years in TV and modeling. I passed the audition and on the 19th June I was offered two DJ jobs, one at a shopping arcade near Marble Arch called Marbles Market, and the other at the soon-to-open Upper Bar Discotheque, which was on the top floor of the Inter-Continental Hotel on Park Lane.

My new boss, R C Gautier, was a well-known DJ from pirate radio with the "handle" or nickname: "The Great Dane." He had a magnetic personality and I liked him, at least at first. Mr. Gautier taught me everything I needed to know about how to DJ. I was soon to discover that being a DJ was, and is, the perfect occupation for me. Because of my problem with spelling and reading I had developed a talent in the use verbal communication. Having the gift of the gab and being able to work with music suits me, partly because the profession of DJ does not require one to be good at spelling.

# LONDON TOWN DISCOTHEQUES LTD

10 BLENHEIM STREET (New Bond St), LONDON W1. TELEPHONE 01-491 7455

RCG/LD

R. Hallifax Esq.,
I Sefton Paddock,
Stoke Poges,
Bucks.

I9th June, 1975

Dear Mr Hallifax,

This is to confirm that you will work as a disc jockey
for London Town Discotheques at Marbles - starting on
Tuesday Ist July 1975 for a fee of £30.00 per week.

Hours I2-6   Thursday I2-8pm

Starting Ist August (approx) you will work at the Inter-
Continental Hotel London for a fee of £40.00 per week.

We will provide accomodation at 4a Addison Gdns for the
month of July.

Yours sincerely,

R.C. Gautier.

VAT NO. 239 8787 94

*Letter from London Town Discotheques.*

"Hi, I'm your DJ, Richard Hallifax live on air at "Marbles Market", playing all your favourite hits, and spinning right now is the hot sound of George McCrae with his super hit record entitled *Rock Your Baby*". Marbles Market, a mini mall, consisted of lots of small shops all under one roof. My job as DJ was to promote items on sale in the "mall" as well as entertain the customers by playing their favorite songs. I worked Monday to Friday from 12 noon until 6pm, and on Thursdays to 8pm for a fee of 30 pounds a week.

London Town provided me with accommodation, which was a basement flat situated at Addison Gardens in the Sheppard's Bush area of London. When I moved into the one-room apartment it was also being used as a storeroom for mobile discotheque equipment. I complained and the equipment was removed. Then, within a few days, I made the place my home.

The Upper Bar at the Intercontinental Hotel London was a prestigious venue. Before the discotheque opened there had been some controversy. From the new night club's huge, tall windows on the top floor of the hotel it was possible to see down to the end part of the gardens of Buckingham Palace. The discotheque dance floor was built like a spaceship with colored lights pulsating from above, and its floor and roof where made of metallic metal. Shortly after the Upper Bar opened, and just when I was settling into the gig, my boss asked me to fly to Hanover in Germany because the resident DJ at the Hanover Intercontinental Hotel had suddenly left and they needed a replacement DJ fast!

I was disappointed to leave London especially having just begun as DJ at the newly opened Upper Bar Discotheque, but the thought of flying to Germany also excited me. When I arrived at the Intercontinental Hotel Hanover I was provided with a room in the hotel and told that I could take all my meals in the hotel restaurants whenever I liked. I was very cocky in those days and thought that I could do whatever I wanted, and I did. For example, it was summer and I wanted to sunbathe, so I put on my small bathing trunks and went outside to the main entrance of the hotel where I lay on a statue which was in the form of a chair. The first thing arriving guests saw was an almost naked man, but I did not give a damn as to what anyone may have thought, I was on top of the world!

Being a DJ in Germany was not quite the same as being a DJ in London; I felt that the roll of DJ did not have the same status. Even though the German girls where very friendly! On the music front, the experience was good for me as I had to play some song's I was not familiar with, music that the German people liked. I did not realize it at the time, but this was very good training for what was to come in my future.

I found the German people to be very kind and friendly and thought it terribly sad that we had to go to war with this country. At the end of the Second World War 90% of Hanover city center was destroyed due to the carpet bombing done by the RAF and the US Army Air Forces. Although I understood why we had been at war, and why it was important to defeat Hitler, I do question the amount of destruction that took place in order to win it. Knowing that Hanover had been almost completely destroyed made me feel ashamed. However, most of the city was rebuilt within a decade. In fact, Germany's rebirth after the war has been described as a miracle.

After a month in Germany I was asked to return to London and continue at the Upper Bar. Upon returning to the basement flat I discovered that my entire record collection had been stolen. Unknown to me my employer had allowed other people to use the flat whilst I was away. My personal records where never returned and for me this was a very hard lesson, which sadly contributed to me having little trust in my boss, and for that matter anyone else.

Despite my records being stolen my boss Mr. Gautier and I had lots of fun together. He invited me to parties at his home and there where many visits to the Hard Rock Café (the world's first) on old Park Lane. Here, I enjoyed drinking Harvey Wall Bangers and eating good food, before taking a short walk to the Upper Bar Discotheque at the Intercontinental Hotel to begin the nightly Disco show.

The Intercontinental promoted the Upper Bar on London's Capital Radio. The advertisement gave the feel that the Upper Bar was "the place to be", and that this is where London's high society chose to spend their evenings. The strategy worked and the Upper Bar did become London's top high society discotheque.

Then I could not believe my luck. Up to now I was the one who had been chasing the girls, trying to find a partner to build a life and family with. As everyone knows this is not an easy task and up to that point in time, although I had been in relationships with some fantastic women, for various reasons, as you have read, the relationships did not last. But here I was, the DJ at London's top discotheque, and for no apparent reason the tables had turned. I was getting offers from the women – they were now chasing me and asking me out! I have never understood why, but on reflection perhaps I was perceived as a celebrity, and that was something women found attractive. In any event the experience made me very mistrustful of the opposite sex. This is also because some of the woman who approached me were in relationships with other people. However I was determined to find a partner I could trust? I thought to myself, why is the world so full of immorality? Even worse, I was being sucked into it too, with temptation all around. For me it was like being on Pleasure Island in the film Pinocchio. In Pinocchio's case he wanted to become a real boy, but had little chance whilst choosing the wrong path. In my case I wanted to get closer to Jesus, but that wasn't easy faced with all the temptation that surrounded me.

The manager at the Upper Bar had a strategy which was to always wait for a queue to form before letting anyone in, even when there was no one in the club. When the first guests arrived via the elevator, he made them wait at the entrance until several more guests had arrived who then joined the line. Their first impression was that the Upper Bar was so popular that to have a chance of getting in one had to join the queue. And for some reason people like to queue. As the good reputation of the club spread, celebrities began to come. Greg Lake from the group "Emerson Lake and Palmer" was a guest and he gave me a copy of his single *"I Believe in Father Christmas"*; I said to him that I do believe in Father Christmas! To which Greg replied that I was the first person to say that to him, referring to his song. Mrs. Alistair Maclean, wife of the Author, was another regular guest, and she and I became friends. On one occasion, after finishing work at 3am, I was invited to her home for drinks. I was driven in her chauffeur-driven Rolls Royce to her apartment in Knightsbridge. When I arrived at 3.30 am, Champagne was served to me on a silver tray by her butler.

In November of 1975 my boss came running over to me whilst I was playing at the Upper Bar. He had just returned from a month's holiday on the Island of Bermuda. He said with great excitement "I have the new thing", "what's that" I enquired calmly, "It's mixing" he said. At the time DJ's played a record and linked to the next song by saying a few words in the microphone. My boss went on to say that when he was in Bermuda he went to a club and the DJ mixed one song into another. I won't go into the full technicalities, but at the time turn tables were slow at the start so one needed a slip mat. By holding a finger pressed down on the record, and then lifting the finger, one released the spinning disc when the turn table had got up to speed. So, the idea of mixing was not going to be easy, but my boss explained that I should play records that sound similar, one after the other; so I gave his idea a try. For example, I played *"El Bimbo"* by "Bimbo Jet" and mixed that song to *"Bongo Rock"* by the "Incredible Bongo Band" and then followed with *"Brazil"* by "The

Ritchie Family". And a primitive form of mixing was invented. From the late 70s direct-drive turntables became more popular to use and replaced belt-driven turntables in discotheques. And this made mixing a lot easier for DJs.

Living and working in London was not without risk. The Irish Republican Army (IRA) was blowing up bombs. On November 18th, 1975, a bomb exploded at Walton's restaurant in Chelsea. Mrs. Maclean was a friend of the owner who, as a show of defiance, had decided to re-open the restaurant as soon as possible after the bombing. The restaurant had not been restored and was still in its bombed out condition, despite this many celebrities attended and I was invited to DJ the event, which I felt to be a great honor.

At last I had found something that I was good at. I was successful as a DJ, and on reflection one of the reasons why is because I have always played requests. Guests would come to the DJ booth and ask if I had their favorite record. I made sure that I had copies of all the records that were likely to be requested, and when I got a request and did not have the record I went out and bought it the next day. Popular songs at the time included hits by Tina Charles with "*I Love to Love*" and Barry White with "*You're the First the Last my Everything*". One request I will never forget is when a young lady with a Swedish accent asked, "Hello do you have a song with "ABBA"". She was interested to learn that my father was born in Sweden. Monika was with her friends, and she invited me to join them for an early breakfast at the Hilton Hotel just over the road from the Intercontinental. Monika and I talked about Sweden, our favorite music, and decided to meet again. One thing led to another and we fell in love, I felt Monika was a woman whom I could trust.

One morning after work I arrived at my flat and realized I had run out of cigarettes. I usually got back at around 4am from the Upper Bar Discotheque and enjoyed a cigarette before trying to get some rest. I had received a letter from a friend in México; in the letter was something that looked like a cigarette. Perhaps it's a joint I thought, but what the heck I needed a smoke. I remembered when the Canadian couple had given me joints to smoke, and nothing happened, so if this is a joint it must be harmless, I thought! I lit up and started to puff, after a while it seemed that the walls in the flat where moving, then things went from bad to worse and I felt that I was going to die. I heard someone knocking on my door, it was Monika, and she was together with her Norwegian girlfriend. I pleaded with them to take me to the police or call for an ambulance. The Norwegian friend examined the joint, giving the impression that she was some kind of expert, and knew what she was talking about. "We had better take Richard to your place Monika" she suggested. Monika drove us to her place, and I crashed out on her bed. The hours passed and soon it was time for me to go to work. I began as usual at 9pm, but every time I spoke into the microphone I began to laugh, and for no reason. At 3am when it was time to go home the manager wanted to speak with me. I thought to tell me I was fired, but instead he told me that I had done my best performance ever. In any event the experience scared the hell out of me, and I have not smoked a joint since.

There were many people from the music business that came to the Upper Bar Discotheque. I was given newly-released records that the record company representatives hoped I would play. "Hi, I'm Ray, see if you can give this a play, and how are you getting home? I've got the limo outside". It was expensive taking taxis, so I was only too pleased to be offered a ride, especially when I was driven in a chauffeur-driven limo. Whenever Ray showed up at the club I was driven home. Ray made friends with everyone, the manager, bar personal and the waitresses.

One Sunday at four in the morning I was woken with heavy knocking on my flat door. I was terrified as the knocking was accompanied by a threatening voice, "let me in, let me in", before opening, I nervously asked from my side of the door who it was. "It's me. Ray, let me in". I opened the door a little when Ray, together with his chauffer, forced their way in. I thought Ray was an odd character; he had a long scar down one side of his face. I had been asking around the music business if anyone knew him, and no one did. "Why are you asking around the music industry about me?" He demanded to know. "How do you know that I've been asking?" I replied. I thought to myself, that my phone must have been tapped. "Well, you told me you were a record producer, but no one in the business knows who you are", I said. Convinced that they were going to harm me I broke down in tears, then for no apparent reason their threatening attitude calmed, and much to my relief, Ray and his chauffer left.

The following day, the manager of the Upper Bar was fired. Why, I do not know. But perhaps his leaving may have had something to do with prostitutes who, according to rumor, may have been circulating in the club looking for clients. Mysteriously, Ray and his chauffer were never to be seen again. I have often wondered if they were undercover private detectives hired to find out if any of us working in the club were involved with organizing professional woman. Or perhaps, where they the organizers? In any event the Intercontinental, being one of the world's top hotels, has its good reputation to protect. So, if anything of the above had been true, the Hotel would have had no choice but to put a stop to it.

When there was no one at the club who could offer me a ride home in a limousine I took a taxi, as I have mentioned before, the club closed at 3am. On occasion, prostitutes who had just been with a client at one hotel were waiting for a taxi to take them the next. I was often asked by these women if they could share my cab; this I did not mind as they contributed to my taxi fare! One time, before I met Monika, an attractive woman asked if she could share my taxi. Not realizing her profession I asked her if she would like to join me for a drink, to which she replied "yes, but you do understand that I am a prostitute", she said, and went on to say that she could meet me out side of her working hours. I politely declined, but found it fascinating how she separated her profession from her private life.

As one entered the Intercontinental Hotel reception area, on the right-hand side was a cocktail bar with a pianist playing. One day, whilst talking to the pianist he asked how much money I made, and I asked him the same question. I was astounded to hear that he was making a lot more money than me; given that the Upper Bar Discotheque was the hotel's "big attraction" I felt I should be paid at least the same as the pianist. I decided to go directly to the hotel manager and ask how much they were paying London Town Discotheques for my services. I discovered that the hotel was paying a lot of money to London Town Discotheques of which I was only receiving a small amount. I raised the question with my boss. On realizing that I had been ripped off and used, I decided to find another job. Another of life's lessons had been learnt. The hotel management made clear that they did not want to lose me, but that their contract was with London Town Discotheques who, apart from the DJ, also rented out the sound and lighting equipment to the hotel. Therefore, for the hotel to employ me directly would have been complicated. In any event, I resigned.

I soon found another company who wanted to employ me as DJ. And that company was Bacchus International Discotheques. My first engagement for them was at "Isabella's Discotheque" in Nottingham. Working in Nottingham meant I would have to be away from Monika as her job was in London, but needing an income I had little choice.

I arrived in Nottingham and went directly to the discotheque "Isabella's" where I was to meet the manager and be shown around the club. Here the DJ booth was on a small stage raised up facing the dance floor. It was designed so that the DJ not only played records, but also danced. I was to perform from 9pm to 2am five nights a week, the manager told me.

Apart from "Isabella's Discotheque" the manager also owned a small hotel which had a pub on the ground floor. As it had been agreed that I was to be provided with accommodation, this was where I was to stay. Strangely my room over the pub had no lock on the door, and when I enquired as to why I was told that none of the rooms had a lock on the door. I found this to be very strange and it was never explained to me as to why this was the case. Apart from no lock, my room consisted of two beds, a wardrobe and a bed-side table, all very basic. Bathroom facilities where separate and shared by all the hotels guests, as was the TV room.

Here's a short story from my time in Nottingham. No, it's not about "Robin Hood", but almost.

In 1976 Isabella's was Nottingham's most successful discotheque; people queued almost every night to get in. The head bouncer, Morris, was a huge man and very professional; any trouble was soon sorted out. We had a two-day break – Sunday and Monday. One morning, on one of our days off work, Morris was kind enough to take me on a drive and show me around Nottingham, after which at around lunch time he dropped me off at my hotel. I went up to my room and noticed that my room door was slightly open. If there had been a lock that would not have happened, I thought to myself. Then, as I took hold of the door handle, thoughts flashed through my mind about a man I had seen in the TV room the previous evening. He had a bad vibe about him. As I began to open the door, I noticed that my clothes had been taken from the cupboard and thrown onto my bed. I stopped for a few seconds before entering completely and as I was waiting a hand came from behind the room-side of the door and pulled me forcibly into the room. I was terrified as there had been reports of a murder near Nottingham. I was being attacked, the man began throwing me from one side of the room to the other, and when he could he was hitting me with clenched fists. My state of mind was one of complete terror, but I began to realize that if was going to get out of this situation I would have to start to defend myself, so I clenched my fist and looked the intruder straight in the eye. Then, suddenly, he broke down crying, and ceased with his attack. It seemed that *he* was now afraid of me. Both shaking and wondering what to do next I suggested that we calmly sit down. He sat on one bed and I on the other. Staring intensely at one another I offered him a cigarette. As we smoked, I wondered how on earth I was going to get out of the situation. I asked "what you are doing in my room?". Then he broke down again, and for some reason told me his life's story, and although it took some time, I listened. I released that he was not a well person and gave him the benefit of the doubt. He said he needed money and that was the reason he was attempting to steal my clothes. I suggested that he should go together with me to report the whole incident to the manager. To my amazement he agreed. For that reason, I asked the manager not to report the incident to the police. The manager reluctantly agreed but told him to immediately leave the premises. Right or wrong I felt that I had made the right decision. It also felt good, being able to forgive someone. For me this was an opportunity to practice good Karma (Karma in Hinduism and Buddhism is the sum of a person's actions in this and previous states of existence and viewed as deciding their fate in future existences).

Meanwhile, in London, my friend Paul Grade had started his own Record Company called P&P Records. Paul wanted to record two of my songs *"White Lines on The Road"* & *"Thank You"*. This meant I would have to leave Nottingham and return to London. My last night at "Isabella's Discotheque" was on Monday the 16th August 1976. I was honoured that Isabella's held a farewell party for me which was a memorable evening as many guests came to wish me well.

Upon returning to London I was pleased to be back together with Monika and moved in with her. She shared an apartment located near to Marble Arch together with several other people from Sweden. Needing our own space, we decided to look for an apartment of our own. It wasn't long before we found a suitable place in Knightsbridge, which luckily had two bedrooms. Apartments in Knightsbridge are very expensive to rent, so in order to generate some extra income we rented out one bedroom to David, a DJ friend of mine. David was a real character; everything about him reminded one of how the upper-class must have behaved a century ago! I trusted David. After I had left my DJ engagement at the Upper Bar Discotheque I was asked if I could recommend someone to take my place, I did, and that person was David.

Having given up my DJ work, at least for the time being, Paul gave me an advance payment against royalties to live off, and over a three-month period, treated me to very expensive meals at almost all of London's best restaurants. Paul did not know that his spending around one hundred pounds a night on our restaurant meals played heavily on my conscience as my father was again unemployed. What Paul spent on the two of us in one night was almost more than my father had to live off for a week or two. I recall thinking how everything in life is relative. Here I was with a member of one of the wealthiest families in Britain and Paul was telling me that his parents were worried about the money!

We recorded *"White Lines on the Road "* & *"Thank You"*, backed by a full string section and top musicians at Strawberry Studios in London in 1976. I am forever grateful to Paul Grade for believing in my music.

# Chapter 10

## The Forests of Sweden

With the recordings of my songs *"White Lines on the Road"* & *"Thank You"* completed, I had to continue to earn a living, so I returned to my DJ work. "Bacchus International Discotheques" offered me a gig to be the resident DJ at the SAS Hotel in Oslo, Norway. Having discussed the offer with Monika I accepted.

It felt good to be returning to Norway. I arrived in Oslo at the end of October 1976.The hotel provided me with a room that was in an apartment block across the road from the Hotel. From day one I began to work in the night club. At the SAS hotel guests, if they so wished, could turn on the radio in their room and listen to the DJ playing live in the night club. And, on occasion, I received requests from guests who would call me on the phone from their room, but sometimes I had to think twice before playing the requested song, as at the same time in the night club guests would be dancing to records like *"Daddy Cool"* by "Boney M" or *"Johnny B Good"* by "Chuck Berry" and playing the requested song may have resulted in an empty dance floor, especially if, for example, it had been a song that people did not generally dance to. But as with my first DJ engagement at "Marbles Market" in London this was very good training for me for the future, if I was to become a DJ on the Radio, which is something I was aiming for. During my free time in Oslo, I took the opportunity to go cross-country skiing and see once again the city's attractions, including the ski jump "Holmenkollen", the "Kontiki" museum and the "Vigeland" sculpture park.

It wasn't long until December when Monika flew over from London to join me in Oslo. The night club was to close for the

Christmas holidays, so Monika and I travelled by train from Oslo to the small Swedish Town of Köping, which lies about 75 miles (120 km) west of Stockholm. Here I met Monika's family for the first time and looked forward to celebrating my first Christmas in Sweden together with them. Celebrating Christmas in Sweden was something I had been looking forward to, especially having listened to my father's memories of how Christmas was when he lived in Sweden as a boy. Dad had wonderful memories how Father Christmas ("Jul Tomte") arrived at his home on the horse-drawn sled in the snow. But he never mentioned the Swedish Christmas food.

It was Christmas Eve and much to my surprise Monika's family began to open their gifts. Why can't they wait until tomorrow, Christmas day? I thought. Then, at three o'clock the whole family gathered around the television to watch cartoon films. I was told that this was a Swedish tradition. After the Donald Duck and friend's cartoon, we sat down for what the Swedes call "Julmat" (Christmas food), but this was the strangest Christmas food I had ever seen in my life! Where is the Turkey? I thought. Instead, there where various kinds of fish including "sill" and something called "Lutfisk", trying to be polite and wanting to give Monika's family a good first impression of myself I tasted a little of the fish and thought it was disgusting. "Now what is this?" I politely asked Monika's mother, "well this is "Janssons Temptation" (a strange potato dish), and this is "julskinka" (ham), there is also "revben" (ribs), red beets and cabbage" she replied in English, but with her charming Swedish accent. All kinds of food that I never knew existed were on the table, and I was told that I could eat as much I liked. Wanting to be polite I did taste a little of everything, but to be honest I did not feel too well afterwards. Luckily, Monika's father offered me schnapps and then we all said "skål" (cheers) several times. I became quite drunk. Fortunately, the Schnapps settled my stomach. Monika's family had gone to a lot of trouble to make this year's "Julbord" extra special and all in my honor. But I was still wondering why there was no Turkey! These Swedes are strange I thought. Although the family did their very best to make me feel at home, deep inside I was longing to be with my family in England. I felt lonely, especially with not being able to understand the language. When everyone laughed, I did not understand what the joke was. It's just a rehearsal I thought, tomorrow on Christmas day everything will be just as Dad had described it would be. But nothing was. Yes, Dad had been brought up in Sweden, but his father was British and probably they had celebrated more in the English way I thought. Then, much to my delight Monika's mother very kindly cooked a splendid turkey, which we all enjoyed for lunch on Christmas day. This was followed by a gift to the family from Monika and me – we announced our engagement. The whole family where very excited with the news, and plans were immediately put in motion for organizing our wedding. What would be a good date? Who to invite? Where would my family, who would be coming from England, stay? And so on, was discussed. Monika and I were only at her home for a few days and it was easier making plans together with her parents whilst we were all together.

Christmas passed and it was hard for Monika and I having to go our separate ways. I had to return to Oslo because the SAS hotel management was planning its New Year's Eve party, and it was important for the DJ to be present to plan the music to be played. Monika had to return to London to continue with her job.

My employer, "Bacchus International Discotheques", had secured a contract with "Sara Bolaget" (Sara Company) in Sweden. "Sara Bolaget" was a state-owned restaurant and hotel chain. One of the company's restaurants was in Gothenburg, a well-known restaurant called "Henriksberg". Bacchus wanted me to become the resident DJ at the restaurant's discotheque, which was called "Nättmössan" ("The Night Cap"). Sweden was not to join the EU until 1995 and in 1977 it was difficult for citizens of other countries to be granted work permits in Sweden. As I was going to marry a Swedish citizen it would be, perhaps, easier for me and my employer's Bacchus knew this.

The timing of when I was to begin my new gig in Gothenburg was perfect and fitted in with Monika's and my wedding plans. We had decided to marry on March the 12th 1977 in the Swedish town called Köping. This was almost a month before I was to begin the new gig in Gothenburg. In Oslo I had made friends with another English DJ and he kindly agreed to stand in for me for the few days I would be away for the wedding.

Monika's family had made big plans for our wedding. They had invited everyone from their large, Swedish family as well as my family and our Swedish relatives. Mum and Dad somehow managed to get enough money together for their trip over from England. In 1977 low-cost air travel was not yet available so they, together with my two brothers, and sister, had to travel by train, bus and on the ferry.

We had a wonderful wedding. The ceremony was in Köping Church and afterwards the reception was held in the local hall. One of the many highlights during our wedding party was when two of Monika's younger sisters acted out and mimed to the song *"Dancing Queen"* by ABBA.

But sadly, it was soon time to say goodbye to friends and family. I felt very emotional. In those days it felt as though England was a long way away, and when my family, who had come all the way from England, had to leave, I had no idea as to when I would see them again. Then, once more Monika and I had to part. I had to return to Oslo and Monika to London. For two newlyweds this parting was not easy so soon after just being married, but both of us knew that within a few weeks we would soon be together again.

My time in Oslo was drawing to an end. A few days before I was to leave there was great excitement at the hotel, this was because the singer Sammy Davis Jr was due. Sammy Davis was in Oslo to perform at the "Chateau Neuf" concert hall. As Mr. Davis entered the hotel, guests, hotel staff, and I filled the lobby to see the star. We got to see him as he made his way from the hotel main entrance and walk to the elevator. I have to admit, that even I found the experience exciting.

Then the day came for me to leave Oslo. I travelled by train to Gothenburg on the 14th of April 1977. I enjoyed the journey, looking out at the pristine forests and farmland as we made our way towards our destination. As the train approached Gothenburg the industrial buildings I had seen before on previous train journeys came into view, and I wondered if I was going to like living in the in the city. But the good news was, that I would soon be back together with Monika.

On my arrival to Gothenburg Central station I hopped aboard a tram and made my way to the restaurant "Henriksberg" located on the street "Stegbergs Liden" and once there I met the manager Stig. He began by giving me a guided tour of the restaurant. On the ground floor I felt that I had walked into Las Vegas; the walls where lined with one-armed bandits (slot machines). The discotheque where I was to work was named "Nattmössan" (the night cap) and was in a large room next to the gambling hall. Then we walked up the stairs to the second floor, and into a first-class restaurant. At one end I noticed a gaming table; here, customers could play roulette and blackjack, and from the windows on the other side of the restaurant guests could look out over the river "Göteälv". I was impressed. As Stig continued with the tour he said, "It's in the contract that you can eat in the staffroom, you will find it in the kitchen area" he said in his best English mixed with Swedish. It amused me when Stig would get his English words back to front, for example he would say "it's my never mind", when he meant to say, "I don't mind".

Bacchus, my employers, had also written into my contract that the restaurant must provide accommodation for me. Having been shown around "Henriksberg" Stig then drove me to where I was to live, when I explained to Stig that I was newly married and that my wife was soon to join me, he replied, "the accommodation is only meant for you". I replied, "no wife, no DJ". He thought for a moment and said, "Ok she can stay". We were provided with a room in an apartment where an older couple lived. Having been introduced to the couple and been given a key to the apartment, I returned to "Henriksberg" and to the kitchen to eat some food. I introduced myself to the head cook and kitchen staff, then for the first time in my life I experienced what it feels like to be treated as an immigrant. The head cook told me that I should return to England! Sweden is for the Swedes he said. I was of course shocked as I had always believed that we Englishman where most welcome in Sweden. I then thought to myself that his words where ridiculous given that my father was born in Sweden and that his mother was Swedish – something the cook did not know. And then I thought how Swedish does one have to be, to be Swedish?

Because of this experience I have strong sympathy for immigrants. It is worth noting that Gothenburg had been built by people from other countries. The city has been heavily influenced by the Dutch, which can be seen in some of the architecture and canals that remain to this day. Also, in the 1800's when the City became more industrial, many people from Scotland arrived to work here and made Sweden their home. Then over a long time many English people made Gothenburg their home too, some became very wealthy from trading over the North Sea. This wealthy, English businessman then made donations towards building the library, university and hospital in the city. Since then, and because of their generosity, Gothenburg is often referred to as little London. My point is that the city to a large extent has been built by foreigners.

As the days and weeks passed, I began to enjoy what the city had to offer, for example the architecture, museums, parks, shops, restaurants, as well as the experience of riding on the trams and I gradually grew to like Gothenburg.

Monika arrived from London; it was good to be back together but living in the apartment turned out to be a nightmare. We couldn't sleep. The couple who owned and also lived in the apartment, had fights, throwing items at one another. We soon realized that they were alcoholics, so Monika and I had little choice but to find alternative accommodation.

It wasn't easy and we were not in a position to be fussy, but in the end we found a place on the outskirts of town called "Bergsjön". I was very impressed with the apartment, the standard on the inside was as high as my wealthy friend Paul Grades apartment in London, and Paul's apartment was luxurious. However, the area that "Bergsjön" is situated in was regarded by Swedes as a "slum". In my opinion, at that time in 1977, "Bergsjön" was as far removed from a "slum" as one could get. I later found out the reason why some Swedes referred to the area as a slum and it was because we, the immigrants, lived there!

One evening at "Nättmössan" I noticed a guest inject something into his mouth; it looked to me as though he was taking some kind of drug. I politely said to him that he should leave. The man explained to me that he was not taking drug's, but something called "snus", at the time I had no idea as to what "snus" was. It is tobacco he explained; you put it under your lip in your mouth. He insisted that I try some, and being the curious person I am, I did; I almost turned green and felt that I was going to collapse. After the experience I decided not to take "snus" again, until years later when I decided to give up smoking and "snus" became a very good substitute.

Then on August the 16th 1977 the news came that Elvis Presley had died. The news came as a shock to his fans all over the world, including me. The Swedish people loved Elvis and from that day I was inundated with requests to play his songs. Song writers Dick Bakker, Eddy Ouwens and Dunhills wrote a song dedicated to Elvis Presley entitled *"I Remember Elvis Presley" (The King is Dead)* and I received requests to play the song several times a night for months.

With its first-class restaurant, dance bands and discotheque, as well as having the added attraction of gambling, Henriksberg was a magnet for attracting people. Almost every night there was a queue of people lining up to get in. In the 70's and early 80's The discotheque "Nättmössan" was on the ground floor of the restaurant, but a few years later it was moved up to the second floor to where guests could view the ships coming and going on the Göteälv (river) as they dined and danced.

One evening at Nattmössan there was a small technical problem, a young man introduced himself by the name of Mats, and he convinced me that he could help fix the problem. Mats became a regular visitor, and often spent time chatting with me. We discussed the idea of starting our own company that would lease and sell discotheque equipment. We could see a niche in the growing discotheque market as it had become clear to us that the international companies had little, or no, understanding of the Scandinavian market, but we did!

Then, having worked in Sweden for several months the question of income tax came up. Bacchus International Discotheques moved their DJ's to different countries in the world after a three to six month period, thus avoiding local taxes. This was all to do with how long one could live and work in a foreign country and how much money one was allowed to earn before local tax became applicable. This meant that, for example, in Sweden, discotheque companies based in the UK could offer very competitive prices for the hire of sound, lights and a DJ because no local income tax would apply.

Because of this situation, and after I had been a few months in Gothenburg, Bacchus wanted me to move to the Hilton Hotel in Cairo, Egypt. For Monika and me this was impossible as we were expecting our first child. I was in a difficult situation and I was advised to seek help from the Swedish musician's union "Musikerförbundet". This I did, and also became a member.

The Swedish Musician's Union works to protect its member's interests and fight for fair and equal pay. With foreign DJ's not having to pay local tax their members were priced out of the market. Because I wanted to remain in Sweden my employers in London, "Bacchus", would have to increase my pay to include local tax, but that had not been priced into their contract with the restaurant in Sweden. Therefore, the Union was only too pleased to help me. A representative from Bacchus was sent over from London. Negotiations between Bacchus and the Swedish Music Union took place and eventually an amicable agreement for all parties was reached. I had now been the resident DJ at "Nattmössan" for almost a year; I was released from my contract with "Bacchus" on the 3rd of March 1978.

So, what now? Here I was in a foreign country married to a beautiful Swedish woman and we were expecting our first child. On the one hand this would be a fresh start for me, on the other all my friends and family lived in England, and to be quite honest, apart from having the company of Monika I felt lonely. It soon became obvious that I would have to try and learn some basic Swedish. So, I went on a three-week beginner's course. In the beginning I found it hard to take the language seriously and I will give you some examples as to why. The word for "drive in", for example into a garage, in Swedish is called "infart!" And to exit is "utfart!" so, as you can imagine, I found this to be hilariously funny! Then there is the word for Labor Union which in Swedish is "Fack!". And "Phus" is for garage parking. Hello in Swedish is the word "hej", which to me sounded as though it was something to feed animals with! Of course, the Swedish language is beautiful, but some words can be amusing to an English-speaking person who is learning it for the first time.

On occasion Monika and I went for a drive to see what the

countryside was like surrounding Gothenburg. As soon as we had driven a short distance from the city we were in never-ending forest. I remember thinking to myself then, as I do now, how beautiful Sweden is with its abundance of nature. During the winter months the forest becomes transformed. It becomes a magical winter wonderland, with virgin, white snow topping the branches of the tall fir trees and gives the impression that everything has been covered with icing, like on a Christmas cake. Then, as spring approaches, and the warm sun causes the snow to melt, and the forest, having received a fresh dusting of crystal snowflakes, looks as though it has been sprinkled with icing sugar which, on a clear day, contrasts against the never-ending, pastel-blue sky.

But there is more, there are over 97,500 lakes in Sweden. The natural beauty of the country and its size, twice that of the United Kingdom provided me with a sense of freedom that I had not felt in England. Breathing clean, unpolluted air, and being away from the crowds of people in London, was for me like finding paradise. I began to dream of one day finding a house of my own in the forests of Sweden.

It is Important to mention that during the late 70's the economy in Britain was not good. But in Sweden it was very good; the country had not been affected by the Second World War as Britain had been. The Swedish standard of living was, at the time, the envy of the world. Also, it was a trendy place to live, partly due to the success of the pop group ABBA and the tennis star Bjorn Borg. And I was now living in a country where I would not be used and abused as I had been in England. At least that is what I naively thought at the time.

# Chapter 11

## Saturday Night Fever

Thanks to the Music Union I was introduced to Claes who was responsible for the DJ's who played on the Stena Line ferry boats that traveled back and forth between Gothenburg and "Frederikshamn", in Denmark, as well as to Kiel in Germany. In those days almost all the Stena Line ferries had a discotheque on board, and that meant they needed disc jockeys. I was offered a job.

On my first day I arrived at the ferry terminal dressed in the latest fashion from Carnaby Street in London. I wore my velvet suit, frilly-white shirt and black, high-heel boots. I carried my boxes full of 45 rpm records onto the ship "Stena Jutlantica", then up the stairs to the bar and discotheque.

On board there was a mix of travelers, some would be leaving the ship in Denmark whilst others where on a day return. My audience consisted of families, businessmen, pensioners, truck drivers, and a few who were interested in music and wanting to dance. I remember receiving requests for every type of music. I found it strange playing a track from Led Zeppelin and then a Swedish folk-music tune followed by a song from the film Saturday Night Fever. Returning to Gothenburg was always party time, most people on board the ship drank far too much and many where stone drunk. When the boat rocked back and forth with the waves and wind it amused me that those who were dancing found it hard to keep their balance and were shuffled from one side of the dance floor to the other as the ship swayed.

The 1st of December 1977 was one of the greatest days in my life! I become a father. Being present during the birth was, for me, like experiencing a miracle. My wife Monika was wonderful, and our first son was born. We had spent some time thinking of names, as all parents know this is not an easy decision to make. After all, our children will have to live with the name we give them throughout their lives. Monika and I decided that we wanted a name that was at the time not very common. We had no idea as to whether our first child was to be a boy or a girl, so we were prepared with both a girl's name and a boy's name. As we had been gifted with a boy, we decided to name him Hans. You will have to read on to know the other choice.

At Stena Line we DJ's would be called to meetings for general updates and information. During one such meeting with my boss Claes we began a discussion on the idea of starting a radio station. Claes mentioned to me that he knew an American DJ, Alex St. John, who was also interested in such a project. In those days, Swedish Radio (public broadcasting), which is Sweden's equivalent to Britain's BBC Radio, was the only radio station on air, and during the 70's played very little in the way of popular music. The only alternative was 208 Radio Luxemburg, which one could listen to during late evening and through the night. Thanks to Claes a meeting was arraigned for all of us DJ's, who had an interest in trying to find a way to start a radio station, to get together. The American, Alex, and I, exchanged telephone numbers and we became friends.

As I mentioned before Sweden had not yet become a member of the EU so when the boats docked in Gothenburg all the passengers and crew had to go through passport control and customs. The crew all wore uniforms and were seldom checked. Ironically, many of the ship's crew had goods which they smuggled in under their clothes. I was dressed in my frilly-white shirt, velvet suit and high-heel boots. Perhaps because I looked different, this was the reason as to why the customs often checked me! On one occasion I was strip searched. Leaving the ship became a nightmare. I never had anything to declare. I explained the situation to my boss Claes, soon afterwards every DJ who worked for Stena Line was provided with a uniform as well as a Sterna Line ID card. Whilst I could see the sense of the ID card, wearing a uniform was not something I thought suitable for a DJ. It quite simply wasn't cool. For me it was the same as asking Jimmy Hendrix to put on a suit! So, I began to look for other ways to further my DJ career. That way of thinking is perhaps hard to understand now, but at the time I lived the part of being a DJ to the full. And to me the clothes I wore were an important part of my image.

Whilst working for Stena Line I had kept in touch with Mats, the guy I had met in the night club. We decided to have a go and start our own discotheque company, which we named "Scandinavian Sound Services". We found a suitable local for an office and showroom on "Karl Johansgatan" street in Gothenburg. Within a short time, we won contracts to install sound and lighting equipment in new discotheques in the cities of Oslo and Copenhagen, as well as Gothenburg. Needing finance, we secured a bank loan. The bank had a customer who manufactured loudspeakers, and we were introduced to one another. Having tested the quality of the loudspeakers and wanting to keep our bank happy we decided to buy our loudspeakers from the firm. This was to be our first mistake. The loudspeakers turned out to be not of good quality; they broke after a few months use. My partner Mats was responsible for the technical side of our business, but as it turned out he wasn't the good technician I had at first been led to believe. This meant that we had to call in professionals to help complete our contracts. And that was our second mistake! The extra costs incurred were to have been our profit. Mats admitted that he was in over his head when it came to the installation of advanced sound and lighting systems. So, he decided to quit. That put my wife Monika and myself in a difficult position. We had an office, a spectacular show room with a show case state-of-the-art sound and light system. We had secured agencies for some of the best equipment in the disco-theque industry, and we had been successful in selling five dis-cotheque installations. But we would now have to take over the share of the bank loan that Mats had secured. Okay in theory, but Monika and I were not in the financial position to do so. So, very sadly and regrettably, without the financial support from Mats or someone else it was impossible for us to continue with "Scandinavian Sound Services". And that was the third mistake, because the discotheque business was just about to take off into its golden age.

As a matter of interest when we left our office and showroom, and the new tenants moved in, I asked why they were putting up posters of men with machine guns. They explained that they were Kurds, and that our old office and showroom was to be the meeting place for their members in Gothenburg! Nice guys though!

With the business venture behind me I continued with my DJ work. In order to get bookings I needed business cards and other printed material to help promote myself. When we had "Scandinavian Sound Services" we had found a printer, so it seemed natural to ask him. His name was John; I liked him as he was quite a character. John was always interested in what I had been up to as he had a strong interest in music. One day he invited Monika and me to a party, and we accepted his kind invitation. On the evening of the party we arrived early at the venue. The entrance door was open, so we made our way into the building. Having passed the entrance hall, we found ourselves in a large reception room. On the left was a very grand stairway leading up to the next floor. But there was no one to be seen, have we come to the right place we wondered. Then we could hear voices coming from somewhere at the top of the stairs, so we made our way up. At the top of the staircase was another large room, there were a few men looking out through the windows, each with a communications device. I enquired as to what they were looking out for, and one of them said "the Police", followed by drawing a gun and pointing it directly towards my stomach. Shaking and feeling shocked, Monika and I were given the instruction to walk slowly backwards down the stairs. The man with the gun following all the time, with his gun pressed into my stomach. Then, just as we arrived at the entrance, our friend John showed up. When John explained that we were his guests the gun was lowered, and we were invited to go up the stairs again. Now, you may be wondering as to why I have shared this bizarre story with you and the reason is that as I stated earlier, my living in Sweden was to be a new beginning, a chance for me to get away from the types of people I had met in England, but that was not to be the case! Since the above incident I have met two people in Sweden who were connected with the night-club business who have shot other people. One, a DJ, walked up to a man in a kiosk, took his money and shot him, and the other, a night-club manager shot the owner of a pizza restaurant just because he was in competition to his business. Yes, during my time in England I did meet some strange characters but none who contemplated using a gun. So Sweden was not turning out to be the safe place that I thought it would be!

The popularity of disco was now spreading all over the world and not least in Sweden. I received offers to play DJ gigs up and down the country. I was in the right place at the right time. And Swedes loved English DJ's. Partly because during the 70's and 80's a high percentage of the hits originated from England and I guess it was exotic to have a native, English-speaking, DJ from London playing the records. In any event I no longer needed to work on the boats, and I could wear the clothes that I wanted too. Best of all, because most of my gigs were at weekends I was free to enjoy quality time together with my young son Hans and my beautiful daughter Heidi who was born on the 31st January 1979.

# Chapter 12

## Free Radio

In 1979 Radio VSD 95 FM took to the air. VSD stood for: "Västra Sveriges Discjokey *Förening*" (The West Sweden DJ Club). We were able to establish our radio station because in 1978 Community Radio was licensed in Sweden. The station was not allowed to finance itself through advertising, so we had to raise funds through sponsorship and donations. In the beginning, Radio VSD rented studio time from the student radio station at Chalmers University in Gothenburg. We broadcast for one to two hours a week. Our idea was to play nonstop pop and rock music presented by our group of Swedish, American and English DJ's; and to introduce to listeners in Gothenburg how music-radio sounds. It was our hope and dream that through our efforts we would contribute to pave the way for commercial radio in Sweden, and that those radio stations would, in the future, employ us. Swedes had previously had the possibility to listen to pirate radio broadcasting from ships located off the coast, The programs were presented by DJ's who played popular, hit music, but sadly the government had stopped these stations from broadcasting, as was also the case in the UK.

We had no way of knowing at the time that Radio VSD 95 FM was to become a legend. I believe this happened because the station not only played hit music but also because of the wonderful personalities who presented the programs. We gave one another nick-names, so for example I was "Lord Hallifax", and one of the stations technicians was known as "Spiderman", referring as to how fast he moved his arms and hands when operating the mixer board. What our station provided was good, clean, fun entertainment with lots of back to back hit music.

At home our family was expanding. On the 27th June 1980 Monika and I were blessed with our third child, and second son, whom we named James.

Later that year, on the 8th December 1980 came some tragic news. It was the middle of the night around 4am when I was awoken by my phone ringing, I lifted the receiver it was my American DJ colleague Alex. Rich I am sorry to wake you, "have you heard the news?" he asked, "no, what news?" I replied, Alex went on to say, "John Lennon has been shot". I was shocked and thought back to when I had met John at "Top of The Pops", that he was so down to earth and easy to talk with. Alex did not know much more so we ended our conversation. Having heard the news I was unable to sleep, and then during the hours that followed I was very sad to hear that john had passed. My colleagues on Radio VSD, knowing that I had met John, asked me to take part in a special radio program. In John's honour we played many of "The Beatles" songs he had written together with Paul McCartney as well as his own such as "*Imagine*".

Now to something that may make you smile. I presented my Radio programs using English as I had not yet bothered to learn the Swedish language, as most young people in Sweden understood English this was not a problem. I loved to receive telephone calls during my live radio program. There is one call I will never forget. The caller asked me if I liked gays, remembering that I had to be very careful with my words and with what I could or should say, I replied that I had nothing against gays and that well, we are all different, and that we must respect one another's sexual orientation, carefully pointing out that I was not gay myself. In the studio control room, our sound technician Rolf "four hands" (that was his nickname) was listening to my response and couldn't stop laughing. Whilst playing a record and with the caller on hold I asked Rolf what was so funny, he explained to me that the caller was referring to a well-known

Gothenburg football club called "Gais". Well, if you didn't know the difference what would you have thought?

Now, I want to share a very special story with you. I am very grateful to my parents for having brought me up in the Catholic faith, and for instilling in me a good sense of what is right or wrong. Despite everything I had been through it is because of my Christian upbringing that I have managed to remain somewhat balanced, and for that I am very grateful.

However, as you have read, I unfortunately did not always follow my conscience, and have, on occasion, taken the wrong path and given in to temptation. Realizing that this was causing me to be unhappy I decided to try and change myself for the better. So how was I going to do that?

First, I prayed that I would meet a Catholic priest with whom I could share my past life and receive some guidance on how to go forward. Then I decided to once again attend mass, and I went when I could on Sundays, to Christ the King church in Gothenburg. After several visits I eventually plucked up enough courage and decided to speak to a priest. One Sunday after mass, I approached the priest who had taken the service and asked if there was perhaps a young priest with whom I could talk. I wanted to meet with a young priest as I thought he might be more understanding when it came to my profession as a DJ.

I was introduced to the newly ordained Father Emmanuel Cordina. Father Emmanuel had a room where we could talk. He offered me a wooden chair to sit on. When I sat on the chair it collapsed and fell apart into small pieces. Feeling embarrassed I gathered up all the wooden pieces and apologized, "that's okay" said Emmanuel, and laughed. When we had collected our thoughts, he heard my confession, and having survived that! He listened to all I had to say and gave me some very good advice.

A few days later I purchased a new chair from IKEA and left it at the Church. My thought is that there is always something positive in all that happens, Because of the chair Father Emmanuel and I have been best friends ever since.

Father Emmanuel loved popular music and very kindly sponsored one of my programs. As Radio VSD grew in popularity we increased our broadcasting hours and the Swedish recording industry became keen to give their support. Apart from presenting the station with the latest record releases in the hope that we DJ's would consider playing them, we were invited to interview artists. There were many interviews, but some of them where extra special. For example, in 1981 I was privileged to interview Stevie Wonder when he came to perform at the Scandinavian Arena in Gothenburg. There was something extraordinary about him; he had an aura, best described as spiritual. I felt this as he placed his hand on my shoulder all through the interview, and for me it wasn't the interview that I remember so much, but more his spirituality.

*Me together with Steve Wonder 1981. Photo Calle Ballonka.*

Then in 1982 I met Elton John who was in Gothenburg to perform at the Scandinavian Arena. A colleague from Radio VSD joined me to take photographs. The recording company representative led us to a changing room at the back of the arena where it had been arranged for us to meet Elton. My college and I prepared our recording and camera equipment, then in came Elton, to my surprise he seemed to be very nervous, which was of some relief to me because I thought that I was the one who was feeling nervous. When I asked my first question, to my surprise Elton began to stutter, but then Elton made a joke about his stutter by saying, "this is why I did not get the film part". My interview with Elton went well, and then when we were ready I mentioned that my Grand-mother was a personal friend of Sir Stanley Rouse "President of FIFA 1961-1974." I knew that Sir Stanley and Elton often met be-cause of Elton's interest in football. The now, more relaxed Elton, told me that Sir Stanley was soon going to visit him at his home in England. I felt that Elton warmed to me; he seemed friendlier, as though I was no longer a stranger who had come to interview him. Elton then asked if my college and I would like tickets for the concert and invited us for refreshments. In hindsight it was silly of me not to have mentioned Sir Stanley before the interview.

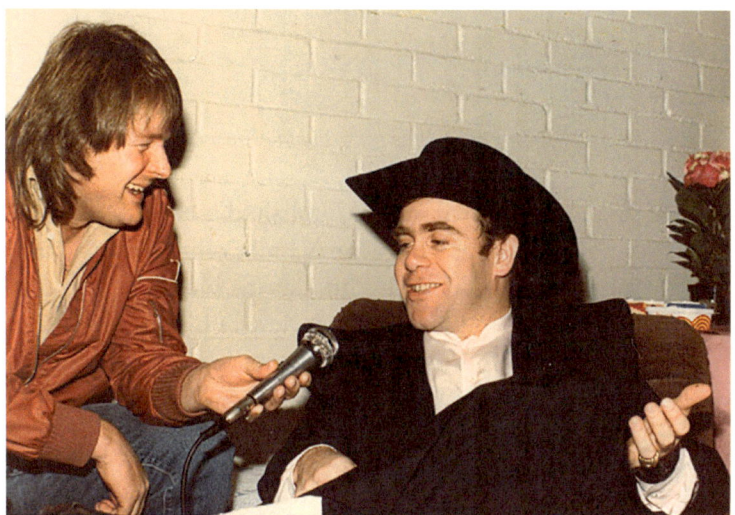

*Together with Elton John 1982. Photo PG Gustafsson.*

Another interview that felt extra special was in 1985 when I met Phil Collins. We discussed everything from how he became a member of the group Genesis to how he found the inspiration to write his hit songs such as *In the Air Tonight* and *Against all Odds*. We also discussed his collaborations with Philip Bailey and Eric Clapton. It was a great interview. And Phil was so generous that he even shared some of his private life with me.

*Together with Phil Collins 1985. Photo Anton H LE Clercq*

My brother Charles owned and published a magazine called "The Skier". Charles was a huge fan of Phil Collins. Hearing how successful my interview with Phil Collins had been, Charles asked me if he may publish the interview in his magazine. For me this was a real opportunity. Having my name in such a well-read magazine might help in establishing my name as a DJ in Europe I thought, so I accepted the offer.

Charles had many contacts in the travel business, primarily in the ski resorts. Because of this he was able to rent villa's for our family at very attractive, low rates. This provided all family members, both in Sweden and in England, with an opportunity to meet up for holidays. One such holiday was arranged in the resort of Crans-Montana in Switzerland, a fantastic place high up in the mountains. When we arrived Charles asked me if I would like to interview the world downhill skiing champion Pirmin Zurbriggen, for his magazine "The Skier". There was just one problem with this. Because I did not follow skiing, I had no idea as to who Pirmin Zurbriggen was! I was therefore totally unprepared for the interview, but I decided to give it a chance and go ahead. I found Pirmin to be a very natural and pleasant person, he was easy to talk with and my interview with him went extremely well. To my surprise I heard from Charles that the readers of "The Skier" enjoyed reading the result. On reflection, the best interviews I have done have been those when I have been least prepared, probably because instead of just asking questions it's been more of a conversation.

Radio VSD was now more popular than ever but the team spirit that had united our team of Disc Jockeys in the beginning had begun to fade. We had allowed our egos to get in the way and there were arguments over how much airtime each of us had.

Then our DJ club "VSD" decided to arrange an event, it was called "Disco Forum 80" and took place on the31st August to the 3rd September 1980 at a venue called "Rondo" in Gothenburg. It was understood that some of the profits from the event would go to help finance Radio VSD. The Swedish recording industry gave the project its full backing. Artists performing at the event included the American group "Village People" who performed their world hit "YMCA". The event was a huge success, and according to my calculations there may have been some money over to help finance our radio station. But if there had been a profit from the event the money was never to be seen, as to where and why and to whom I do not know, but this caused me to fall out with some of my colleagues and my interest in the DJ club rapidly began to diminish.

One evening, after my radio broadcast I received a call from a man who said that he wanted to meet me regarding a project to start up a local TV channel in Gothenburg. The project sounded interesting, so I went to meet him. I listened intensely as he made his presentation. "How will you finance the station and secure a license?" I asked. He explained to me that the new local TV station would broadcast under the same regulations that applied for Community Radio in Sweden. I had an idea for fund raising for Radio VSD, but had not shared my idea with my DJ colleagues, due to my mistrust of some of them.

For some crazy reason, I decided to take a chance and share my idea with this stranger, in the wild hope that I may be offered a TV program of my own, should he get the TV project of the ground. I proceeded to explain the following idea. In Sweden it is permitted for sports clubs and other non-profit organizations to sell lottery tickets and offer a prize, as long as the prize is not cash. Radio VSD and the new TV project were community-broadcasting projects and came under the same rules and regulations as the sports clubs in Sweden, with regards to lotteries. The Radio and TV stations could sell lottery tickets to raise funds, and the draw could take place during a live broadcast, which would encourage people to tune in to the Radio or watch the TV program as they would want to know if they had won a prize. The man listened intensely and asked me what I would want in return should he proceed with my idea. I replied, my own TV program for one year. I thought to myself that if my program had not been a success within a year there would be no point in continuing for a longer time. Not taking his TV project to seriously, I wished him luck and left.

# Chapter 13

## Touring DJ & Record Producer

For over 100 years people in Sweden have gone out to enjoy music and dance in their local Folk Park ("People's Park"). These venues are literally to be found all over Sweden, many of them are out in the open air; perhaps in an area in the middle of a forest, or fields ringed by a perimeter fence with a wooden stage at one end. Some are more developed and have the appearance of very large village halls. During the 60's, 70's and 80's pop groups and DJ's would often be booked to provide the entertainment at these parks. The Beatles, Frank Sinatra, ABBA, Chuck Berry, and the rock group ACDC are amongst the countless artists who have performed in Sweden's Folk Parks. When I was booked to play as a DJ in the parks I sometimes played for the entire evening and was the main attraction, and on other occasions I would play records for an hour or two and then introduce the band. Thanks to these parks and their popularity I was able to earn a good living during the eighties as a DJ in Sweden.

Whilst playing in one of the parks a group from Gothenburg called "Perhaps" caught my attention as they reminded me of ABBA. The group had two girl singers, backed by three guys. Liking their sound, I asked if they needed a manager, and they did. Shortly afterwards I arranged for the group to record a song which we wrote together, the name of the song was *"Playboy"*. I had a very good relationship with a record company called "Sonet Records", in Stockholm. I was confident that "Sonet Records" would listen to the group's demo and they did! It wasn't long before we received a positive reply from the record company, and I was invited to Stockholm for a meeting.

"Sonet Records" agreed to finance the single and suggested that we first record the song in Gothenburg. Needing a studio, we had learned that the legendary guitar player "Bosse Winberg" – a member of the instrumental group "Spotnics", had built a studio in the loft of his house. Bosse was happy to help out. Whilst recording *"Playboy"*, Bosse added his unique guitar sound to the recording. The result was great, and we felt that we had a potential hit record.

I sent the master tape to Sonet. The record company liked what they heard, but wanted me and the group to travel to Stockholm to record some extra instruments, in their studio.

*"Playboy"* by "Perhaps" was released on the Sonet record label on the 11th June 1980. The song received good reviews and was played often on radio stations up and down the country as well as in Finland.

I worked hard as manager promoting "Perhaps" and we teamed up for a tour. I was the DJ and Perhaps the live band. The group were on their way to success, but for any group or artist to have a chance of "making it" in the highly competitive and overcrowded music business, requires focus and absolute dedication. The group members had day-time jobs and taking holidays was, for some members of the band, more important than touring. This meant that sadly, despite all the effort, the group's career was short lived.

But I had not given up on releasing my songs *"White Lines on the Road"* and *"Thank You"*. So, I registered my own record label in England called "Fax Records". My friend Paul Grade had decided not to proceed with his own label in the music business and was only too pleased to help. He gave me the master tapes for *"White Lines on the Road"* and *"Thank You"* and in 1979 the "White Lines on the Road" single was released for the first time.

Then Monika and I wanting to get a family pet decided to get an Old English Sheep Dog. Looking back this was of course complete madness, given that we had three small children and that we lived in a very small flat, but at the time it seemed like fun. The name of our dog was Snoopy, and he was the most loving dog one could wish to have. He put up with our three small children climbing on his back and pulling on his long, white hair and he never complained. But Snoopy was a big dog and he took up a lot of room. Needing more space Monika and I decided to look for a house. Wanting a safe environment for our three children to grow up in we decided to look for a house away from Gothenburg and out in the countryside, preferably with a large garden. We could be flexible when it came to location as my DJ work was not at any one fixed location. After viewing several houses, we found a place in the middle of the forest not far from the village of Dalstorp, which is located approximately 69 English miles east of Gothenburg. Our new home had the fitting name of "Skogsglantan", which means "the house in the wooded glen". The nearby village had a school and some shops, and there was a large lake with a sandy beach.

As it turned out It was a very good thing that we had moved from our small apartment in Gothenburg to a house. On November 15th, 1982 Monika and I were blessed with our fourth child and third son and we named him Sebastian.

I felt a sense of freedom living deep in the Swedish forest, compared to my previous homes in and around London and the concrete block of flats where we had lived in Gothenburg. Here, the children could play in the large garden and forest that surrounded the house, climb as many trees as they wished, make as much noise as they liked, and live in a clean environment. During the summer months of July and August we could swim in any one of the many nearby lakes, and during the winter go skiing and tobogganing, as well as build snow men in the snow. There was an abundance of wildlife, which included animals such as moose and deer that would often wonder through the garden and come close to our house.

But we were not alone! There were other families with children within walking distance a few hundred meters or so away, who had also decided that living in the natural environment was preferable to city life. And there was another added advantage, the school bus collected the children from each of the family's' houses and brought them home again. Knowing my family was safe and secure was a good feeling for me when I was away doing my DJ work.

It is worth noting that quite a few of the local people where "blind" to the beauty that surrounded them, for them their dream was to live in a big city. They could not understand why I preferred living in the forest as opposed to living in London.

Have you ever tried something and that no matter how hard you try you just cannot make it happen, but that you refuse to give up? Well that is how it was and is for me regarding my song writing. After years of trying without success I had not given up. On the 26th July 1983 I put plans in motion for my new record label which I named "Superfax Productions". This came about because I had noticed potential in a group of young musicians whilst judging a talent competition, and they needed a manager. So, within a short time I signed the group for management, recording and publishing. The name of the band was "Crazy Visions".

Not owning a studio of my own to record in I hired the legendary "Studio Bohus". The studio was located on the west coast of Sweden, not too far from a Town called Kungälv. "Studio Bohus" was well established; artists such as "ABBA" and "Status Quo" are amongst many who have recorded music at the studio. The studio employed a talented sound engineer, "Åke Linton" His talents contributed to the production of several of our recordings.

The group's first single, with the A-side title "Beauty Queen", and on the B side, "Back to Rock´n Roll", was released in 1980 followed by another A side release: "Crazy Nights" and on the B side "Let's Make Love", in 1982. Then in 1983, we released "The War is Coming", which became the group's biggest hit, played on almost every radio program in Sweden. The song was also a top hit on the radio program "Europatoppen" and was also used for a national TV campaign to remind people to vote in the Swedish General Election that was held in August 1985. Also, in 1984 we recorded the song I had written at the age of 16 for my friend Chips sister *"Mr. Man in the Moon"*

At the time the idea of filming music videos was new. I was approached by a production company called "Visuell Kommunikation" who, having heard the song *"The War is Coming"* on the radio, wanted to make a video, which the company would then use as an example to show to their potential, new customers. This was of course an opportunity not to be missed. I agreed to the idea and asked if they might be interested in filming a second video for *"Mr. Man in the Moon", to which they* agreed, and two pioneering videos were made.

Needing a distributor to get Superfax productions records out to the shops I reached an agreement with the record company "Sound of Scandinavia". Then, just as things were going right and "Crazy Visions" music was being played on radio stations all over Sweden "Sound of Scandinavia" went into liquidation. Luckily, in April 1985, I received confirmation that I could retrieve almost all of the "Superfax Productions" records that remained in their stock. However, now having no distributor meant the records were not going to be in the shops. So, with that the venture came to an end.

But, as I have mentioned before there is always something good with everything that happens, even though we may not see it at the time! That "Sound of Scandinavia" went into liquidation of course was not good news for me, but for my cousin Neville living in England it was a blessing in disguise. Neville had dreams of becoming a pop star; he had written some very good songs and found a manager to represent him. His manager had flown over to meet with me hoping that I would help Neville secure a record distribution contract, at least for Scandinavia.

So some weeks before "Sound of Scandinavia" had gone into liquidation" I had presented them with the idea that they distribute Neville's records. They loved Neville's songs, and then just before we were all going to sign an agreement the news arrived that the company had ceased business. This sadly meant that I was not able to help my cousin. But that was in fact the blessing! because not too long afterwards Neville decided to not use his birth name for show business, but go under the artistic one of – "Belouis Some", and he signed a recording deal with EMI Records in England, had he signed a deal with Sound of Scandinavia it may have compromised his chances with EMI Records. Belouis Some went on to achieve several world hits, his most successful with the title *Imagination* was recorded in 1985.

That same year on the 1st April 1985 "Crazy Visions" and I parted company. The group decided to change their style from being a young rock band to becoming a dance band. Dance bands during the 80's and 90's were in high demand in Sweden, so it was easier for the group to earn a living, but if I may say so, not nearly as much fun as being a rock band! But as a dance band with the name "Tiffany" the group achieved success. and we have remained friends ever since.

Thankfully I was still in demand as a DJ. My gigs took me all over Sweden and sometimes to Oslo in Norway where I played at the popular discotheque "Teach Inn" on Peder Claussensgt Street. When in Oslo I was also often invited to be a guest DJ on the legendary "Radio Ung".

# Chapter 14

## *Disco Dynamite!*

A family from Denmark had moved to our local village Dalstorp and taken over the local restaurant, which had the name "Pensionat Haga". The family and I became friends; what we had in common was that we had moved to the area from our respective other countries. Whilst the local people where very kind and friendly it was not easy to feel accepted coming from "the outside". And it was said by some, that it would take a generation for an "outsider" to be fully accepted by the local community.

John was a chef and he had some very good ideas as to how to attract people to his restaurant. One was to organize a Disco. He called me with the idea of setting up a partnership to arrange the "Disco Nights". We agreed, and once a month, just after the local workers got paid, would be the best time. John and I got along well; we made a success of our "Disco Nights", which became very popular with the local community. One reason for this was that people did not have to drive home after having a drink or two. Most of our guests lived within walking distance of the restaurant. John and I came to an arrangement where I took the entrance money and John took the income from sales of food and drinks. Other costs for a guard and advertising where shared between us.

My DJ career continued to go forward in a straight line. A friend of mine, "Sir Charles" also a Disc Jockey, had made friends with the American representative for the "Pepsi Cola" company who was in Sweden to establish the brand. "Sir Charles" introduced us to one another and shortly afterwards Pepsi sponsored me, paying for my posters and other promotional material holding a can of their drink. Pepsi asked "Sir Charles" and me to make a promotional music cassette for the company. But Pepsi were not my only sponsor, I had another company called "Tanner Jeans". During the spring of 1984 "Tanner Jeans" wanted me to do a promotional tour for them in Finland. They arranged for me to travel by ferry from Stockholm to Helsinki followed by a tour of Finland's east coast. Everywhere I played in Finland there were crowds of people. The young Fins treated me as a major celebrity. Whilst in Helsinki one of the country's top radio presenters "Tapani Ripatti" from "Rund Radio", the "Finnish Broadcasting Company", invited me to present a half hour radio show to be broadcast nationally. On returning to Sweden I was delighted to receive letters from listeners in Finland saying how much they enjoyed my program.

Then, in Sweden on the 17th May 1986 I was asked to help arrange an event to raise money for children suffering from cancer. It was to be held at "Boråshallen" (it is worth noting that "The Beatles" played at this venue in 1963 before an audience of 2,500 people).

Some of Sweden's most successful groups and artists of the time agreed to take part, among them was the group "Style" who had just won third place in the Swedish music competition "Melodifestivalen" with their song *Dover Calais* ("Melodifestivalen" is a program that is produced by Swedish Radio/TV, to select the song that will represent Sweden in the Eurovision song contest).

I was delighted that the group wanted to take part as they where hugely popular and would draw a lot of their fans to the event. I was told by their record company that the group was booked to appear in the Swedish town of "Skara" during the afternoon on the same day that we were to arrange our event. Knowing that the group was available in the evening I came up with the idea of flying them from "Skara" to Borås in a helicopter, some 67 miles. My wife Monika managed to get her boss who was a wealthy and successful business man to agree to sponsor the cost of the helicopter. The record company's representative Stuart spoke with the group and they agreed to the idea. Stuart added that another Swedish star "Pernilla Wahllgren" would also love to come. When the helicopter landed there was an added surprise as Pernilla had the company of her boyfriend Emilio Ingrosso . Screaming fans came to greet them as the helicopter landed. It is of interest to note that 32 years later, in 2018, Pernillas and Emilio's son Benjamin Ingrosso represented Sweden in the Eurovision song contest in Lisbon, Portugal with the song "Dance you Off". The event I helped arranged raised lots of money for children suffering from cancer and was a huge success. I am grateful to everyone who took part.

With the event behind me I went back to my DJ work and continued touring in Sweden. At almost every place I played, finding a parking space wasn't always easy, sometimes the only availability was at some distance from the discotheque. I would then have to carry my heavy record boxes along sidewalks, and upon arrival to the venue I frequently had to carry the heavy boxes up and down stairs, and if that wasn't enough more often than not an architect had designed the DJ booth and had given very little thought to the realities and needs of professional DJ's. Having the mixer board and turn tables in the right position, with enough space for records to sit on a shelf at the right height, was important.

Luckily, there was one discotheque that had everything just right. During the 80's I played on a regular basis in the town of Trollhättan (located 46 English miles north of Gothenburg). The discotheque was called "Slussen"(The Lock) aptly named because of the nearby dam, waterfalls, locks, and the hydroelectric power station in Trollhättan, which is described as one of Sweden's seven wonders! Tourists love to see the 300,000 liters of water per second being released into the river. Paul Sahlin was the owner of "Slussen". Paul himself was a well-known singer who, for some years, was Sweden's answer to Britain's pop star "Garry Glitter". Because Paul knew "show business" he made sure that everything was just right for the DJ's and the artists he booked to appear at his club. For example, I could drive my car right up to the back-entrance door of the club and park, then walk just a few strides and be on the stage in the well-designed DJ booth. Also, there was a dressing room and toilet just two steps away from the stage. The night club dance floor looked just like the one in the film "Saturday Night Fever", and there was a metallic tunnel leading into the discotheque from the main entrance. For me as the DJ working at Paul's night club was like real "disco dynamite".

My touring schedule included many appearances on the west coast of Sweden. One town in particular was a favorite of mine, and that was the town of Varberg (situated about 47 English miles south of Gothenburg). Here I loved to DJ at two venues "Societetsparken" and Nöjesparken, the latter was my favorite; here, hundreds of young people came to dance, and I was honoured when they voted me as their favorite DJ.

Surviving as a professional DJ was very hard work. I had to make a success of every gig. It was important to get along with everyone, play the right music ensuring that everyone danced and had fun, so that I would be invited again to play, month after month, and year after year. When things were going well my phone rang nonstop, then there were periods when everything went quiet. Needing help with bookings I engaged an agent, his name was "Spike". I am eternally grateful to Spike. Without him it would have been much harder for me to secure enough work to make a living. Spike booked me primarily to play at the "Baldakinen" chain of dance restaurants, best described as Sweden's equivalent to the Mecca dance halls in the UK during the fifties and sixties, but on a smaller scale. Spike also booked me to play as DJ at many other well-known restaurants including "King Creole" and "Heartbreak Hotel" in both Stockholm and Gothenburg.

One of Sweden's most well-known radio and touring Disc Jockeys, Claes af Geijerstam best known as "DJ Clabbe", was also a musician and sound technician as well as a personal friend of the members of the group ABBA. He was an important contact for me to have and we kept in touch. I remember one of our telephone calls in particular. I lifted the phone to call him, and without dialing I heard his voice, we were calling one another simultaneously which we both found to be such a coincidence. Claus wondered if I would be interested in a gig at the Grand Hotel in Stockholm. Over 500 American students from the "Young Presidents Organization" where coming to the event which was to take place on August the 12th, 1987. I accepted Claes offer. When I arrived at the Grand Hotel, I went to the dance salon to do a sound check and noticed police, together with sniffer dogs checking underneath the chairs and tables. I asked if there had been a bomb threat, "no" they replied, we are doing a security checkup because the King and Queen are to attend this evening's dance. Claes, why didn't you tell me?

The Americans had a ball. The King and Queen sat together with their entourage. Queen Silvia accepted many offers from the Americans to dance whilst King Carl Gustav remained seated.

I decided that I must try to have someone take a photo of me together with the King. Having played and presented records for the first half of the evening, I then introduced the live band. During my break I approached His Majesty and cheekily asked him if it would be okay for me to put my arm around him for a photo. His majesty said nothing and waved his arm as to say no. I took a step back and signaled to the waiter who held my camera to take a photo, which now hangs proudly on my wall.

Then I was invited to DJ the opening night of the new American bistro "Heartbreak Hotel" in Stockholm. The bistro was on the ground floor of the dance restaurant "King Creole" and featured a bar named after the Swedish singing star "Gerry Williams". There was a restaurant and a DJ booth, but there was no real dance area. I had been asked to play rock and roll hits, the owners thought that guests would be happy just to listen. I introduced myself and played the first record, something with Elvis as I thought his music would be a good start and immediately people stood up and danced, then the manager came running over and told me to tell the guests to sit down. He explained that the restaurant had no license for dancing. I continued to play songs by Chuck Berry, Jerry Lee Lewis and The Rolling Stones. Now how do you stop people from dancing to rock and roll songs like that? I couldn't. The next time I played at "Heartbreak Hotel", the owners, realizing that their guests wanted to dance, had obtained a permit for dancing and installed a dance floor.

# Chapter 15

## Satellite Radio & TV

In 1987 satellite broadcasting had arrived. This opened-up a whole new world of opportunities for me to find work presenting TV and radio programs. I was asked by "The Scand Video Group" (a TV production company based in the city Borås) to present a news program in English. The program was called "Sweden Today" and was broadcast in 19 European countries as well as Hong Kong, Kenya, and China.

I decided to "seize the moment" and wrote to several of the new satellite channels, one of them: "Super Channel", had a program called "The Coca-Cola Rock File". The program included interviews with new pop artists, fashion designers, and tips on where to find trendy restaurants and bars. The program featured a different European city each week. In October 1988 I received a telephone call from the producer of the program, who said that they wanted to do a program from Stockholm and asked if I would be interested in making all the arrangements. Having accepted the offer, I got to work and, on their behalf, hired a film crew and arranged interviews with a new upcoming pop group, and a fashion designer. The program was also going to include a feature on Stockholm's most trendy night spot. Having made all the arrangements and fixed the date for filming the program, I arrived in Stockholm and went to the hotel where I was to meet the producer, presenter and film crew. The film crew arrived on time, but there was no sign of the producer or presenter. I waited for around an hour, but nobody turned up. I began to worry as I had planned the whole day. Then at last the producer showed up. She apologized for arriving late explaining that her flight from London had been delayed and then went on to say that her presenter was stuck in Amsterdam due to fog.

"Richard, would you do the interviews", she asked. "Well okay", I replied, knowing that I was totally unprepared. "First, we are going to meet the fashion designer "Marcel Marongiu", and then a new pop duo called "Roxette", I said, and off we went. My first interview went well with the fashion designer, Marcel, and then it was off to interview "Roxette". When we arrived at the address given to me by their record company, I thought that there must have been a mistake because the building looked dilapidated and the surrounding area like a dump. But surprisingly, this is where "Roxette" were rehearsing for their forthcoming tour called "Look Sharp". But once inside the building everything looked very impressive. The stage was built up on two different levels; on one level, a row of guitars mounted on stands and all brightly decorated in different colours, and higher up a magnificent drum set with symbols that sparkled in the strong-coloured spotlights that illuminated the stage. "Roxette" was a duo comprising of two, well established, Swedish pop stars, Per Gessle and Marie Fredriksson, Per's forte was song writing as well as performing, but it was Marie's voice that provided the magic touch. I had met Per Gessle before, so I felt at ease meeting him again, but it was my first time in meeting with Marie. As I mentioned before I was not prepared for any of the day's interviews and regrettably I had not had the chance to listen to "Roxette's" new album "Look Sharp" so I had to do some quick thinking as to how I was going to conduct the interview. I made the decision to do the interview as a presentation of Per and Marie for the European audience who, at that time, had not yet heard of "Roxette". The program was broadcast Europe-wide on the 27th November, 1988. Not long after, "Roxette" had their first world-hit single entitled *The Look*.

*Together with Roxette 1988. Photo private.*

Another high point was on midsummer 1988 when my colleague DJ Clabbe invited me to be his guest DJ on his program "Rakt over Disk". The program was broadcast nationally on Swedish Radio P3. As Clabbe played mostly disco and dance music I decided to be different and chose to play nonstop rock and roll hits; some of the records I played were "Dire Straits", *The Walk of Life*; "Status Quo", *Caroline*", and "The Rolling Stones" with "*Satisfaction*".

# Chapter 16

## Radio 7 Your Way to Heaven

During the spring of 1989 I was asked to present a radio program for tourists on the local Swedish Radio station P4, Radio Jonköping (Sweden's equivalent to BBC Local Radio). Jonköping is situated at the southern end of Sweden's second largest lake, Lake *Vättern*, and lies almost in the middle of the southern part of the country between Gothenburg and Stockholm. I knew the town well as I had made regular DJ appearances in many night clubs and discotheques in and around the area over many years.

The station asked me to present my program in English and play music of my own choosing, now what could be better than that, I thought, so I jumped at the opportunity. My program soon became popular not only with tourists, but also with the local population. Recognizing the popularity of the program, the station manager asked me if I would like to continue with the show after the summer season. But, he added, on the condition that I present my programs in Swedish. This presented me with a problem as up to then, I had stupidly not bothered to learn the language, apart from the few words I had learnt on my beginner's course when I first arrived in the country. My excuse for not having tried to improve my Swedish was because my audiences in the discotheques, as well as those who booked me, expected to hear me speak in English when presenting my live DJ show. After all, I was the DJ from England!

The solution was for me to prepare everything I would say in English and have my wife Monika kindly translate everything to Swedish. Once in the studio for my live broadcast I would attempt to read my Swedish script, in the end I mixed up the two languages and spoke what is referred to as "Swinglish". Apparently the listeners loved it, because for them it sounded exotic and rather funny to listen to.

My program needed a name and after many suggestions it was decided to call my radio program "Heta Vax med Hallifax" (Hot Wax with Hallifax), which in some way referred to the vinyl records I played being made from wax! Of course records have nothing to do with wax, but the name sounded good in Swedish when linked to my name Hallifax.

I was my own producer, presenter and sound engineer. I played hit records based on chart hits in England the USA as well as from Sweden. The songs where linked together with jingles and I encouraged my listeners to take part in lots of competitions. I also presented the program at a very high tempo compared to the other programs on the station. "Heta Vax" became so popular that in 1990 another station, "Radio Sjuhärad" in the town of Borås, also engaged me to present my program.

"Heta Vax" took to the airways in Borås on Radio Sjuhärad, better known as Radio 7, in the summer of 1990. I remember my first broadcast well because the station manager Pe Ge Johansson told me that at 3pm I was to move a fader on the control bench to connect the station to the national news broadcast. But at 3pm I was so into my program that I completely forgot. Thankfully no one seemed to mind. During the broadcast I came up with the phrase "Radio 7, your way to heaven".

My two radio programs on the two local stations where broadcast from June 1989 until June 1991 on Radio Jönköping, and from the summer of 1990 until August 1993 on Radio 7.

During 1993, Radio 7 asked me to rename my program to "Guld med Hallifax" (Gold with Hallifax) and target an older audience. This meant that for the first time I was restricted when it came to me choosing the music I felt I should play. The station wanted me to focus on playing "Golden Oldies". That's fine, but from my point of view at the time, this made me feel like a caged lion, no longer having the freedom to mix old and new music together, and based on what I knew was popular when playing to live audiences at dance restaurants and discotheques. Yes, "Gold with Hallifax" was a popular program for which I am grateful. but I have always felt that my first program "Heta Vax med Hallifax" had that extra something.

*Live on air at Radio 7 in Borås Sweden. Photo private.*

*Presented for celebrating 100 broadcasts on Radio 7 in Borås Sweden.*
*Photo private.*

# Chapter 17

## Halifax versus Hallifax

When I first came to Sweden in 1997, I soon realized that my family name Hallifax was unique in the country. I had made enquires to find out if I should register my surname in some way in order to ensure that I and my family maintained the exclusive rights. I was informed that in Sweden when a family name is unique, it is automatically protected by law. So, I was surprised when I received a letter on the 16th February 1988 from a company with the name Halifax that was based in the town Jönköping. Now In case you have not noticed my name is spelt with double L "Hallifax" and the registered company with one L "Halifax". The company had to by law ask me to give them permission to use the name Halifax as a trademark. But how they managed to register the name as a company name I did not know, so I sort legal advice, and was told that the company's registration dept (Bolagsverket) must have made a mistake and that If Halifax AB will not free willingly change their name that I would have to take them to court. Also at the time Halifax AB was a newly registered company that sold advertising products.

As you have read, during the 80's I was a well-established DJ in Sweden and often played in the town of Jönköping, not only on the radio, but also in the town's night clubs and discotheques. My name, Hallifax, was constantly being advertised in the local papers as DJ Richard Hallifax, sometimes spelt with one "L" and sometimes with "LL". Hard to hear or notice the difference. With my radio programs on Radio Jönköping and the publicity that came with my live appearances it meant that, at the time,

I was quite well known in the area and it was clear that people identified the name Hallifax with me.

Guests in the discotheques where asking me about the new company I had started "Halifax AB". Strange I thought, as I had not registered a company using my family name and found it odd to hear the question. Besides, I had my own plans to sell merchandise such as T-shirts and caps with my name Hallifax on them. There was obviously confusion between me and the company Halifax. Because of this reality I decided to make it clear to Halifax AB that I would not agree for them to register Halifax as a trade mark, and at the same time I asked them how on earth they could have registered the name Halifax as a business name without first asking my family for permission.

I made a telephone call to Halifax AB, and in an effort to have good relations I offered to buy from them the T-shirts and promotional items I had planned to use myself. This was because I understood that they would endure extra costs when having to change their company name. I thought that perhaps we could work together towards an amicable solution. But my offer was flatly turned down.

On the 5th February 1990 Hallifax AB and I met in the local court in Jönköping. On the 23 February 1990 the court decided in my favor. Then there was an appeal and again I won, and then the matter went all the way to the highest court in Sweden. In the end Halifax AB had to change their name, and they did.

Well, you would have thought that would be that, but it wasn't, the so called Halifax- Hallifax case) was debated in the Swedish parliament.

Although I had won the case in the courts, some journalists in the media seemed to take the side of the other party; obviously not fully understanding my side of the argument, or the court's decision. This I felt damaged my career somewhat at the time. As an extra security I then registered my name as a patent in Sweden and this I did on the 15th June 1990.

# Chapter 18

## Satellite Radio

Satellite television became available during the late 80's and as soon as it was possible I decided to purchased a parabolic antenna (satellite dish), at the time it was unusual having such a huge, round object in the garden, and people passing by would have been forgiven for thinking that we had something to do with NASA. The family now had the possibility to watch programs directly from England and from around the world; for me as an Englishman living in Sweden it was great being able to view the same programs that my family and friends watched in England, and when we talked on the phone we could relate to something we had experienced together. "Did you see that program last night, yes wasn't it good?"

RTL, Europe's largest broadcasting group was one of the TV Companies sending programs via satellite. RTL owned 208 Radio Luxembourg. At the time 208 Radio Luxembourg was the only commercial radio station to reach Sweden and most of Europe, the station was very popular! but it was only possible to listen to the station during the night. The station's signal was sent from the world's most powerful privately owned transmitter using 1,300 kW, broadcasting on the medium wave from the country of Luxembourg.

I thought that perhaps it might be technically possible to send sound without pictures, via Satellite, thus providing all to have the possibility to listen to the great 208 Radio Luxembourg twenty four hours a day! So I wrote a letter to Maurice Vass, who at the time was managing director of 208 Radio Luxembourg London Ltd. Maurice wasted no time in replying and invited me to meet him in London. Maurice liked my idea and presented it to his board of directors.

Then on August the 15th 1990 RTL International (208 Radio Luxembourg) entered the Radio Satellite age. My reward for my idea was that I became the station's link to Sweden. I hear you! (Is that all you got Richard), well yes! but it was better than nothing! So every day from Monday to Friday, early in the morning, I waited for a telephone call from the DJ on duty at the Radio Luxembourg studio. All the stations Disc Jockeys were great, but there was one in particular who I became friends with, albeit on the phone. "Hi Richard, it's Bob Stewart, you're live on air". Bob Stewart is a Radio DJ legend and it was always exciting, fun and a privilege to receive his calls.

I read out my report on the weather as well as all the latest news from the world of entertainment in Sweden, information which I had carefully prepared by reading the Swedish evening newspapers the night before. The hard part was to be sounding awake when the call came in, because I often had arrived home just a few hours earlier at 4am, after a gig. At the same time the children, who were getting ready for school, and the dog, had to be kept quiet. After the broadcast I enjoyed long, private chats, with my DJ colleagues who had nothing better to do with their time in-between playing records in the Luxemburg studio.

RADIO LUXEMBOURG LAUNCHES SATELLITE STATION

Radio Luxembourg launches a new English language daytime satellite radio station on August 15th. The rock and pop station RTL-International will be directed at Scandinavia but the million or so British homes with Astra satellite dishes will be able to pick it up. It will be the first opportunity for British listeners to hear a Radio Luxembourg service during the day.

Both RTL-International and Luxembourg's evening service (established 56 years ago) will be broadcast in top-quality digital stereo on Astra Channel 13, and the evening programmes will also continue to be transmitted on medium wave.

RTL-International will open at 5am and run through to 7pm, when Radio Luxembourg will take over until 3am.

For more information please contact either Steve Wall, Head of News and Press or Jeff Graham, Head of Programmes, on 071 493 5961.

7th August 1990

RADIO LUXEMBOURG (LONDON) LTD · 38 HERTFORD STREET · LONDON · W1Y 8BA · TEL: 071 493 5961 · FAX: 071 409 1643 · TELEX 263912
DIRECTORS: LORD HARMAR-NICHOLLS B.T. J.P. (CHAIRMAN) · MAURICE VASS (MANAGING DIRECTOR) · COMTE J.-P. DE LAUNOIT · J. RIGAUD · G. THORN · J. FELTEN
INCORPORATED IN ENGLAND NO. 50045 · EMPLOYMENT AGENCIES ACT 1973 · LICENCE NO. SE (A) 1777 · VAT REGISTRATION NO. 239 0942 51

*Press release Radio Luxembourg.*

# Chapter 19

## *TV Producer & Presenter*

Now before I continue with my story, which now takes us once again into the world of Television, something far more important happened on the 27th July 1992. Monika and I were blessed with our fourth son, and fifth child, whom we named Justin.

During the same year I was asked to produce and present a TV program for a new local television channel that was based in Gothenburg: "Kanal Goteborg". The TV station had been enjoying instant success; this was because of their program called "Bingo Lotto". "Bingo Lotto" was based on nonprofit organizations such as football clubs, or almost any kind of sports club, selling lottery tickets. Sports clubs were quite willing to sell lottery tickets as it brought in much needed income for their clubs. For every lottery ticket sold, a percentage of the sale went to the club. Then those people who had purchased a lottery ticket would not want to miss the TV program because they wanted to see if they had won a prize. Sounds a lot like the idea I presented to that man all those years ago, don't you think?

I was asked to meet the managing director of the local TV channel who seemed to be well informed about my experience from both Radio and TV. He asked me if I would like to produce a program, which was to be broadcast live on Friday nights. I accepted the offer and suggested a format, which was based on pop music and my idea was accepted.

For the first week or so at the station I had to wait for an office to be allocated to me, so I worked in a corridor. I had a small table and chair as well as a phone. I began by calling everyone I knew in the Swedish recording industry and told them that there was to be a television program where their artists could perform, be interviewed or appear on a music video. This was, for the record companies, a golden opportunity.

It did not take long until I was given an office as well as two assistants, Perra and Anna. It was a priority to come up with a name for the program so the three of us brain-stormed and in the end decided that "Kraft Stationen" (The Power Station) would be a good name. Having decided on the name we needed to make a short film that would be used for the introduction for the program. Arrangements were made for me and a film team to visit one of Sweden's atomic power stations. The "Ringhals" nuclear power plant is located about 65 kilometers (40 English miles south of Gothenburg). Special permission was required for us to enter the plant for filming; this was given as it was an opportunity for Sweden's nuclear power industry to receive some much-needed, positive public relations. And what could be better for them, than to be seen on a TV program that young people would see. However, I would like to make it clear that although I am not in favor of nuclear power, I felt comfortable with our intro film as it had no political agenda! And the power plant turned out to be the perfect location for our film clip. The result was exciting and fun to watch at the beginning of the TV program. Our film from the power plant was clipped together with footage taken from a helicopter flying over Gothenburg. We added sound which included a countdown 10, 9, 8, 7, rather like a rocket launch at the Kennedy Space Centre.

On the 4th Sept 1992, "Kraft Stationen" was broadcast on the local TV channel in Gothenburg for the first time. The program included competitions, pop music videos, dancers, as well as interviews and live appearances with well-known artists. Queues of people waited outside the studio in the hope of being part of our live audience. Guests on the program included the group "One More Time" and, as a point of interest, one of the group's members, Peter Grönvall, had a very famous dad Benny Andersson from the group ABBA, all very exciting at the time! The group "Ace of Base" had just released a single with the title "*All That She Wants*". Our program was the first to interview the band and play the song, but the group had made a promise to a station in Stockholm that they would be first, we honoured the group's wish and waited a week before broadcasting our interview, but after all this time I can now confirm that it was in fact myself who had the first interview.

Artists would often visit Stockholm and their record companies would arrange for them to be interviewed by the media in order to promote their latest record or tour. Producing and presenting the TV program meant that the record companies had me high on their list. This meant that I got to meet and interview many artists for the program, including the American group "Bon Jovi", and the rock group "Cracker". But one interview stood out from the rest; on the 24th of August 1992, I flew from Gothenburg to Stockholm to interview Bob Geldof. Meeting Bob was special. We discussed his band "The Boom Town Rats" his arranging "Live Aid" and his album "*The Happy Club*", although we had never met before I felt as if I had known him all my life and that he was spiritual. He had an aura around him which perhaps he might not acknowledge himself, but I could see it and feel it. Years later, and unexpectedly, Bob was the first person in the world to like my artist sight on Face Book!

Our TV studio was nothing more than a converted night club, a far cry from the studios I had worked in at the BBC. The one thing remaining from its night club days was the bar, which was used to serve drinks to artists and guests who were appearing on the station's programs. The sound and camera crew also enjoyed a beer or two before and after my program on Friday night. This I didn't mind as everyone enjoyed themselves and I felt that it helped the program to go with a swing.

*Together with Bob Geldof Stockholm Sweden 1992. Photo private.*

But word got out that the technical crew drank a pint or two whilst working on my program. Drinking on the job was something the management did not approve of and consequently the bar was closed.

Then disaster struck. Some young kid in the audience had a knife and stabbed another member of the audience during our live broadcast. The Police and ambulance where called. As producer I had to make the decision as to continue the show or not. The last thing the TV station needed was for the press to find out. As we used the same studio as the very successful "Bingo Lotto" program this was all the more important! "Bingo Lotto" was at the time Sweden's most popular TV program and was broadcast nationwide. In spite of the stabbing, I decided that the show must go on. Luckily, viewers at home did not notice anything, and fortunately the knife injury turned out to be not too serious.

Although I was complemented on how I handled the incident, the TV station became concerned about the risk of having so many young people attracted to the program and thinking that perhaps another incident might occur decided to discontinue the program.

Although short lived the success of the program was made possible due to the support we received from the Swedish music industry as well as the talents of the stations great technical crew. But I give special thanks to my assistant's Perra and Anna, who did an outstanding job. Never have so few achieved so much with so little. I say that because any other TV program such as ours would have required a production team of twenty to thirty people – we were only three.

Then in 1993 Gert Eklund, who ran "Kanal Göteborg", started a new channel called TV 21. He asked me to produce two programs "UP to 21" and "21 +". The concept was that the first hour from 8pm to 9pm I presented a pop-music program with videos, interviews and a live band targeting the teenage audience, but without a live audience in the studio! And from 9pm a program targeting young adults with features on fashion, makeovers, news on local entertainment, interviews with celebrities, as well as bands and artists performing live in the studio.

Apart from the above I also produced and presented a special program for the station. On the 12th March 1993 we linked up with the local Gothenburg Radio Station "Radio City" and did a feature on the group "Depeche Mode". For this program the TV management had to give way and allow us to have a live audience. This was because we and "Depeche Mode" wanted the event to be something special for their fans. During the live broadcast our studio audience could chat with the group via satellite from London.

# Chapter 20

## Commercial Radio Comes to Sweden

In 1993 the Swedish government finally allowed for commercial radio to be established throughout the country. Licenses were auctioned off, but sadly the sale was based only on who had the most money, and no thought was given to program content. This is different to the UK where program content can be more importance than how much one pays. So In the UK one can bid almost nothing and still win a license. But in Sweden because being granted a license was only based on who paid most meant that we, who had worked so hard and campaigned for commercial radio, had little or no chance of competing for a license, as we DJs did not have the cash! It was the large, well established media companies that were prepared to pay whatever it took to win a license. The irony was that many of these companies were based in other countries and had little or no idea of how the Swedish market worked, or what it was that people in Sweden like to listen to regarding program content. And, for reasons I will perhaps never understand why these companies did not have the common sense to employ those of us who lived in the country and had the know-how and local knowledge regarding the Swedish market. I thought that with all my experience one of the new stations would offer me a job. But that was not to happen.

Sweden was heading for a financial crash. During the early 90's interest rates rocketed. For a house owner in 1992 with no fixed mortgage the interest could be as much as 24% over a three month period. With the economy slowing people could no longer afford to go out to restaurants and nightclubs as often as they did before. Advertising revenue for TV and radio stations declined. Also, with the availability of satellite TV, video games, and other new technologies, there was plenty of entertainment at home. The consequence for me was that my programs on both local TV and radio came to an end, and my DJ bookings almost dried up.

But, as with everything in life there are two sides to the coin. On the one side, the situation I found myself in allowed me to have more time at home with my family, but on the other, due to lack of income, Monika and I could not make financial ends meet and this put pressure on our relationship. If you have ever gone through financial stress you will know how it is.

Hoping to find employment on one of the new commercial radio stations I wrote letters, made telephone calls, and asked friends in the business for help and advice, I tried everything I could think of, but came up with nothing. Then, finally, as I was about to give up, I found a radio station that wanted me. Well, so I thought.

I left for Stockholm with a heavy heart, on the one hand looking forward to the launch of the new radio station "Bandit Rock", and on the other I did not want to be away from my family.

On the 1st February 1994, Bandit 105.5 the "Rock Home of Stockholm" took to the air and my time slot was from 9am to 12 noon. I was overwhelmed; I received many phone calls and faxes from listeners in Stockholm, mainly from people who had previously lived on the west coast of Sweden and had moved to the capital and remembered my Radio and, or, TV programs.

My American bosses at "Bandit Rock" gave me the impression that they had not had too much experience with Radio in Sweden. Their vision was that "Bandit" should sound "American". I knew from my experience in Sweden that it would be important to use both the English and Swedish language, if their concept was to be accepted.

I thought it was great that I had received so many positive

messages during my first broadcast on the station, but my impression was that my new colleagues did not like it.

Also, it seemed that the Americans did not like my style of presenting; explaining how they wanted me to sound, I was loaned a cassette tape with a radio program from the US, "listen to that Richard that is how we want you to sound". On day two I arrived at the station and following instructions tried to present my program as instructed, but felt very uncomfortable, being rude to listeners is not my style, they called it attitude! Clearly this was not going to work, so we shook hands and I returned home.

During the years that followed "Bandit Rock" was bought and sold several times and eventually became a success. Even though things did not work out for me on the station, I am, to this day, proud to have been the second DJ on air at "Bandit 105.5" the "Rock Home of Stockholm".

On returning home I came up with an idea. One of my children James was a good ice hockey player and the family enjoyed watching him play. But although Ice hockey in Sweden was exciting to watch, the presentation was dull compared to the ice hockey matches that we watched on satellite TV from the USA. Desperate for some income I produced a CD full of jingles and sound effects in the hope that the Ice hockey clubs would buy and use to lift the "presentation" of their matches. And they did. Most clubs in Sweden bought a copy and thankfully the project brought in some much-needed cash.

# Chapter 21

## Event Organizer

In spite of everything my phone continued to ring with offers for live DJ work, albeit less than during the 80's. Needing to find a way to top up my income I decided to have a go and arranged disco events for young people. The name of my new project was "Party Zone". Needing a venue, I rented a very large hall in the village of Nittorp, not too far from where I lived in Dalstorp.

I booked bus companies to collect, and take home, teenagers wanting to come to my disco event. I advertised on the radio as well as in the local papers and I set up posters everywhere I could within a radius of about 19 miles (31 km) in every direction from the dance hall. My objective was that the experience of coming to "Party Zone" was to be something "extra special", an experience one would not forget. I hired the best sound and lighting equipment available as well as the best DJ's and pop groups I could afford. If I may say it myself, the result was impressive.

In Sweden there are strict rules and regulations for arranging dances, especially dances for young people. In order to have a permit I had to make sure that my events where alcohol free and that for every 100 people that there was a licensed guard.

I held "Party Zone" once a month, with great success. Almost 700 young people paid to come every time, but there where another 100 that climbed over the fences, trying to come in without paying, and so there went my profit. There were many who just hung around outside and drank alcohol. "Party Zone" was alcohol free so they were denied entrance. For some reason some parents thought it was my responsibility as the organizer, and not theirs as parents, that their children drank alcohol and for this I was criticized in the local press. It is worth noting that in Sweden some parents tend to think that the authorities are the ones that have responsibility for their children, and not themselves.

After all the expenses for advertising, employing guards, and renting the venue there was little money over. Then, in November 1995 came a blow. There was a huge snowstorm; trees were blown over, power lines cut, telephone lines down. I had no choice but to cancel the event that was to take place the day after the storm. I had expenses for radio and newspaper advertisements that I had paid for as well as arranged for a pop group that was coming all the way from Malmo (a city in the far south of Sweden). I was snow-bound at our home in the middle of the forest. Fortunately I had a car phone; it may be of interest to note that my car phone was too big and too heavy to move, and was therefore screwed into position between the car seats, but at the time it was considered quite flashy to own such a device. It was lucky for me that I had a phone that worked and was able to call from my car to ask the local radio stations to put out a message that the event had been canceled. I reached the pop group who had already left Malmo and told them to return home.

I thought to myself that by using all the negative publicity from cancelling the event and then turning it to something positive I could hold the event a week later and perhaps attract even more people, I would have to give it a go or find myself in debt. Within a week, the weather had improved, and the event was a huge success.

Organizing events comes with risk. Everything must fall into place including the weather. For me all the stress, together with the financial risk, was too much to bear so I decided to discontinue with my venture.

# Chapter 22

## *Never Say Never*

So, what to do now? I was 47, father of five and together with my wife Monika we had a large mortgage to pay. Facing the reality of my situation, as I could see things at the time, I had two choices: one, return to England and attempt to find work on a commercial radio station or two, remain in Sweden and take any job going. I preferred the first choice, but this was not realistic, because Monika had a good job in Sweden and the children were settled in their schools too.

During this time, I spent a lot of time thinking and I remembered what an actor colleague had once advised me. I was asking him about a relationship I was in at the time and told him that I really did not know as to what I should do; to end the relationship or not. And he said that if you do not know what to do then do nothing. Well, it wasn't going to be easy to do nothing, I said to myself, because when it came to be earning a living and providing for my family I had to do something, the question was what. I was a DJ and the idea of doing anything else was not on my horizon, but faced with reality I had to be prepared to try something else I thought.

But what other kind of work could I possibly find? At the time there was high unemployment in Sweden. I remembered when driving through our local village Dalstorp, on my way to gigs, I could not help but notice the factories. I remembered saying to myself I will never work in a factory again, thinking back to how it was to work in the paint factory in England before I became a DJ. However, I needed extra cash so after long debates with myself I decided, reluctantly, to call the local industries and ask if there was a job for me, at the same time hoping there wouldn't be any. I thought, well, if I at least tried to find work my conscience would be clear.

Then in April 1997 I received a telephone call. It was the human resources manager of a local company that made parts for the automotive business. I recognized that voice I thought. It was Kenneth whom I had previously employed as a guard at dances I had arranged. "I did not know that you had a daytime job working as human resources manager at the factory", I said. Kenneth replied, "I hear you are looking for work, come down and I will show you around". Shit, I thought to myself, "Yes of course when?" I replied, not really wanting to go.

Kenneth showed me around. I could not believe what I was seeing, the conditions inside the factory were as if I was having a nightmare, the place had almost no windows, the walls where made of grey concrete. The workers all looked alike, dressed in the same blue trousers and protective shoes, each wearing a t-shirt, some so worn out that they had holes in them. There were production lines, press and welding machines that gave out sparks and loud sounds. I thought that I had entered hell on earth.

"Could you begin on Monday?" asked Kenneth. I returned home in a panic. What was I going to do? Noticing one of my neighbours I stopped the car and asked for some advice. "Max, I've been offered a job, should I accept it?" I asked. Max knew I needed work and without hesitation replied, "take it". Then, having considered the matter I decided to give it a go, well it would only be for a few months I thought. DJ gigs where still coming in, albeit not so many and I will soon be back on the radio I told myself.

On Monday the 14 April 1997 I began my new job at the automotive factory at 6:30 am sharp. I was now a metal worker and my starting pay was 75 Swedish Kronor per hour. I was to work

40 hours a week and be paid every two weeks. First, I was given my blue working overalls, and then I was shown to a production line where the company produced steering columns for tractors. I was introduced to the team leader who immediately put me to work assembling parts. I felt deeply embarrassed as the very people who had listened to my radio program, or who had come out to dance and knew me as a DJ, were now seeing me working on the factory floor. What do they think of me now? I thought.

I want to point out that when I became a DJ in England it was regarded as "something great". I was never asked "and what is your day-time job?", whereas in Sweden I was often asked "and what is your real job?", so in retrospect people in Sweden thought nothing of it that I was going to work in a factory. Also, in Sweden there is virtually no social, class system, at least not on the scale that exists in Britain.

During my first few days, a man from another part of the factory came by and asked if I had a brother, I replied "yes, I have two brothers, why do you ask?", "well" he said, "I was wondering if one of them was on Radio Luxembourg", to which I replied "that's me"! This he found it hard to understand, that he had been listening to me on the Radio Luxembourg satellite service and now here I was working alongside him on the factory floor.

As hard as it was for me to face up to my new reality. I understood that if one is going to survive in this world one must be prepared to adapt. Thankfully my new work friends where very kind and accepted me, in fact I think they thought it fun having a DJ on their team.

At work I was not the only one who had taken the job out of necessity. Steinunn, a charming lady from Iceland, had also previously worked in another profession. Luckily for me Steinunn also loved music. I enjoyed our conversations which were often about Beatles music. One day she said, "Richard I want to share a secret with you, please do not tell the others as they will not believe me". She continued to tell me about a pen friend she had when she was a young girl in Iceland. That friend was Paul McCartney. At the time I did not know as to whether I should believe her story, but I trusted Steinunn and decided to give her the benefit of the doubt.

Steinunn is, to this day, a personal friend and she has given me her consent to share this story with you.

Needing a project to feel good about, and finding her story interesting, I decided to try and put her in touch with Paul. Remembering how I arranged interviews and tracked down stars for my radio and TV programs I made a plan. First, I did some research on how to find the telephone number to Paul's Record Company MPL Communications in London, but that was harder than I thought, so I took a chance and called EMI at the Abbey Road recording studios in London. The receptionist put me in touch with a studio technician who kindly gave me the number to MPL. I called and shared the story with their receptionist, and she said that if I could Fax it to her she would pass it on to Paul. This I did on the 29th of July 1977.

I then informed Steinunn so that she would not be shocked; in the unlikely event that Paul should call her. Some weeks passed and I had almost forgotten about the whole thing when Steinunn arrived to work in a state of shock. "He called, he called", she said with delight, and told me all about their conversation. Paul was delighted to reestablish contact with his childhood pen pal, and he asked Steinunn to tell me that my job in the factory was just as important as his. Now, you might think as I did – that's ridiculous! But Paul is right. The reality is that all work, be it yours or mine, is just as important as his, and I thank Paul for his message as it helped me feel a lot better about myself.

Throughout my life God has always guided me, especially when I have been most depressed. There are always lights in the darkness and I got to see one of those lights when, out of the blue, an article about me appeared in a newspaper called "Göteborgs Posten", with the headline "DJ,n som hänförde" (the

DJ that thrilled). The journalist who wrote the article referred to her finding my idol photo in her box of saved memorabilia and recalled loving and listing to my programs on Radio VSD when she was a young girl. Reading the article gave me a much-needed uplift as I realized that my time on the radio in Gothenburg had meant something to someone, and that person is Marlin.

My initial work contract at the factory was for a limited time, during which I had to prove that I would arrive on time, work hard, and get on with my fellow workers. My temporary contract was renewed three times and then on the 22 January 1998 I was offered permanent employment.

Life on the production line was very hard work. Quite the opposite of the glamorous life I was used to in the world of entertainment. Assembling steering columns, understanding instructions, operating machines, lifting heavy items, and in those days, breathing in metallic particles was all part of the daily routine.

It was January 1998. The Metal Union called all of its members in the factory to a meeting, whereupon the factory came to a complete standstill. We were almost a hundred men and women who looked up at our union representative who was standing half-way up the steel stairs that led up to the company offices. We stood in silence to hear what he had to say.

"I have some very bad news" he said, the company is in financial trouble and many of us may lose our jobs. I thought to myself, I have only just begun my new job and here we go again! I looked at my fellow workers and could not help but notice the depressed faces; fortunately, a week or so later the company had found a way to survive and carried on.

I decided to make the best of my new job and focused on doing everything to the best of my ability. There can be no doubt that my colleagues and I manufactured the best steering columns on planet earth. Well that's what we thought! And, as the weeks went by, I found it a little easier to accept my new situation, in spite of the fact that I was not happy. One of my fellow workers could clearly see this and remarked, "Richard you have ended up in the wrong place".

I had been a member of a union since I first worked in television in England. To qualify for employment as an actor at that time one had to be a union member. So, in 1968 I became a member of "British Actors Equity". Then, in Sweden in 1979 I became a member of the Swedish Musician's Union. Consequently, when in 1997, I was invited in the factory to join the Metal Union it seemed the natural thing to do, but I decided to wait until I was offered full time employment before joining. Becoming a member of the Metal Union turned out to be a very good thing. Within a short period of time I was elected to be the vice chairman of the union in our factory. In Sweden the Union has the right to be represented on the company Board of Directors. The Board meetings were held in the English language. As I spoke fluent English, I was the natural choice for the union to send to these meetings. It was the 22nd March 1999 when I was elected to represent the "blue collar workers" on the company Board, and I was also invited to join the management production meetings. My new responsibility required me to attend meetings during normal working hours; the good thing for me was that I now spent less time on the production line. In the board room I was treated with the same respect as all the other directors, however, I did not feel that same respect whilst working on the factory floor where I was "just a worker". I believe the feeling I had was from my prospective, and that if one were to ask the management team, they would say we have always seen Richard and the other workers as the same as themselves. But sadly, there is a difference, I know, as I have experienced both situations.

Representing the Union and having some input about the running of the company provided me with much needed mental stimulus. However, the extra responsibilities did not increase my pay. In fact, it may have had the opposite effect as companies do not want to encourage union representation. A good thing was that because of agreements between the Union and the Swedish companies, union representatives had some job protection, especially the chairman, who was last in line to lose his or her job should the company need to lay people off. Another good thing was the Union wanted its elected representatives to go on lots of courses. I received education on how to improve my negotiating skills, and how to help people in distress such as addicts, as well as to counsel people who had lost their job. Also, knowing about the rules and regulations provided me with an advantage when negotiating on behalf of the Union with the company.

I was to discover that the experience I had gained through working in TV and radio, as well as learning how to read audiences in night clubs, had provided me with useful communication and social skills. This, combined with my previous business experience, helped me to balance my responsibilities as a union leader on the factory floor as well as being able to contribute in a sensible way at the management level. However, I also felt that the Metal Union was an organization that lived in the past. Times have changed since a worker would spend his or her whole life working in the same factory. In modern times people came and went and made career changes during their lifetime. Due to the financial turbulence experienced in recent times well-educated people, and those previously employed at the executive level, have had to, on occasion, accept working for a time on a factory floor, or take other kinds of work that they would not otherwise take. Therefore, in modern time's those of us who have worked, or are working on the factory floor, have a mix of different political views. Workers are no longer born into socialism. A more modern approach would be for unions to be politically free, and to support any ideas from any party that furthers their members' interests.

If adapting to life on the factory floor wasn't hard enough for me, there was to come something even more difficult for me to deal with. Monika told me that she wanted a divorce, and that she had found someone else. For me this came as a complete shock.

I decided to do everything I could to keep the family together, and suggested to continue with our marriage, but Monika was not to change her mind. This meant we had to sell our home in the forest. Since we had first moved there, we had extended the house twice and made massive improvements, with much of the work done with my own hands. We had also bought land in the forest that surrounded the house. For me our home was a paradise and where I had planned to live for the rest of my life, but sadly I did not have the financial means to pay the mortgage alone, and for that reason I had no choice but to agree with Monika and sell the property. Our home was sold at a financial loss. Once again in my life I had ended up with absolutely no money! Needing a place to live I found a house for sale that was not too far from the factory where I worked. One of the good things about living in a village with a small community is that everyone knows everyone. The local bank knew me and trusted me, for that reason I was able to secure a 100% mortgage to buy my new home.

Monika then married her new man. I never imagined that I would be able to forgive her, but with time I did. In the words of the singer "Sting", "*if you love someone set them free*". I realized that in order for me to be able to forgive her, I would first have to forgive myself. I was first going to have to learn to love myself. For me to be able do that I was going to have to practice my Christian faith. It was from that point on that I would go forward and be ready to love again.

We humans are made up of mind, body and soul, and all three need to be kept healthy. I recall seeing a television program with the "Dali Lama" where he answered a question about religion. I believe he said words to the effect of: that all religion is good; he compared the different religions in the world with the different medicines and treatments we need when our bodies are not well, we need to have the correct diagnoses and the right medicine in order to be cured. It is the same with religion; we each need to find the religion that is best suited to each of us in order to keep our soul's healthy.

I have come to realize that mind, body and soul all need to be kept in balance too. Perhaps it does not matter which road we are on as long as the road we take leads us to God. Some roads are long and winding, and others straight. I am not trying to preach! The above is a summary of my own deep thinking!

When I moved into my new home I was not alone, at least not at first, but it wasn't long before all our children moved out. Now they were young adults, they wanted to begin lives of their own. Justin, our youngest son, lived with me at weekends and with his mother during the week.

As for me, having gone through the entire trauma of Monika leaving, then having to give up my dream home as well as having to go to a job to which I was not suited, made me feel very depressed. But what I had been through was nothing compared to what was about to happen in New York.

On the 11th September 2001 came the news that was to change the world. My phone rang. It was my brother Charles calling from Chile in South America where he lives. "Have you seen the news?" he asked. "Switch on to CNN, you will not believe it." I watched in horror as the second plane hit the World Trade Center. I was in shock and worried if there would be war.

Then 11 days later I celebrated my 50th birthday together with family and friends. My brother Charles, unable to come all the way from Chile, gave me a fabulous birthday present. Charles knew that I was depressed and thought a trip to Chile would do me good. Because he owned a travel company he had many contacts in the travel business, and he arranged for me to visit him in Chile almost for free.

Four months later, on the 23rdJanuary 2002, I set off on my journey to Chile. My flight route took me from Gothenburg to London, then onto Atlanta in the US, and finally to the capital city of Chile, Santiago. I was of course very excited, this was my first trip to the Southern Hemisphere, but after such a long journey I was extremely tired and on top of that I was suffering from tooth ache. Charles met me at the airport and from there began my adventure. Having spent a few days in Santiago seeing the sights we then travelled north. Chile is a very long country 2,653 miles from north to south, so during my three-week stay it was not going to be possible to see the entire country so we therefore decided on traveling only north. If I were to write about my time in Chile it would be a book in itself, but to give you some idea, places we visited included "Zapallar", which is a beautiful seaside resort; the "AURA" Observatory high in the Chilean Andes, and the Atacama Desert in the north, which is one of the driest places in the world. But it was my experience at the "Elqui Valley" that I will always remember the most. Since my arrival in Chile my tooth ache had gone from bad to worse, in fact the pain was excruciating and was taking the fun out of the holiday. As we drove through the "Elqui Valley" I felt that I was surrounded by positive energy, and mentioned that to Charles, and he told me that we were in an area where people say they have seen unidentified flying objects; I gave him a strange look as we continued our drive, but he clearly wasn't joking! Despite my tooth ache I made a joke and said that I would love to meet an alien in the hope that their technology would fix my tooth. Well, we did not meet any aliens, but we did find a church. We went in and I said a prayer, and when we came out of the church the first thing we saw was a van with a sign that read dentist. We knocked on the door, which was opened by a man standing dressed in a white overall, and behind him stood a nurse – we had entered a mobile dentist surgery. The dentist understood English, so it was easy for me to explain where I was from, which tooth hurt, and ask for help. I was invited to sit in the operating chair and the dentist kindly fixed my tooth. Alien or human it did not matter to me; all I know is that God answered my prayer!

# Chapter 23

## A New Start

My trip to Chile had charged me with new energy. I was ready to move forward with my life. Dalstorp had been my home for over 20 years. I loved the surrounding nature, the never-ending forests and the lake. I enjoyed my walks by the river (Jälmån) and crossing over the river on the hanging bridge. I had good friends and kind neighbours who, when celebrating a birthday or wedding, often invited me to DJ. But living on my own was not my thing. My children had all settled in the nearby town of Ulricehamn. Realizing that I was lonely they encouraged me to do the same.

Ulricehamn is a picturesque town situated between hills on both side of the lake (Åsunden). A good description of the area would be to call it "little Switzerland". One Sunday, whilst on a walk in Dalstorp I did not see a single person and this helped me to make my decision to move. I sold my house and moved on the 30th June 2004 to a top floor flat at Nillasväg in Ulricehamn. The apartment block is high up on a hill and my flat being on the top floor provided me with a panoramic view over the town and the lake. The only negative with the move was that I now had a long drive to work, which meant getting up each workday at 4.45am.

In Sweden many apartment blocks have a central, communal room for washing linen; the washing and drying machines are usually installed in the basement and are available for all residents to use. Once a week I went down to the basement to do my washing. There were instructions on how to operate the washing and drying machines and a note reminding one to clean up.

One evening I noticed a very attractive woman standing at the wash room doorway, she looked like a "saint" to me as her light-brown hair was lit up by the sun's rays that shone through the washroom window, which created an aura of light around her. If not a "saint" then perhaps an "angel", one might have thought! Wanting to start a conversation, I asked how important it was to clean up, her response was wonderful, but added "please do not to tell anyone what I said". Then she vanished.

It was summer so after work and at weekends I would sit on my balcony and soak up the warm, evening sun as it set over the lake and the hills beyond. I had two pet budges for company who sat in their cage, and I hoped that they felt a touch of freedom when out on the balcony. One evening a kitten appeared from under the wooden partition that separated my balcony from my neighbours, he or she must be interested in my pet buggies I thought. I leant over the balcony rail and passed the kitten back to a man. Then the kitten returned, and I handed it back, but this time to a woman who looked like the attractive one I had seen in the washroom a few days earlier. "Thank you", she said, "that's my son's kitten "Hippy". "I am sorry she's so much trouble, I believe we met in the washroom" I said. "Yes" the woman replied, "and how did the cleaning go?", she asked. "Fine" I replied, and added "was that your husband I had handed the kitten to a short while ago?". "No, I am not married" she replied, "that man is my mother's husband, they are just visiting". I thought to myself, that's good news, I had again met the beautiful woman from the washroom, and she lives next door! I replied "no trouble, I like cats. By the way my name is Richard and you are?"

Eva was single and had been so for several years so I decided to invite her over for tea, she accepted, then she invited me back, and slowly we got to know one another, and yes I began to get that feeling, you know that tingly feeling when you have feelings for someone.

Then one evening whilst driving home from work I crashed

head on with a Moose, which Swedes call "Elk", my car was a complete right off, and the caved-in windscreen almost crushed my face. Covered in blood I called Eva, whose profession is nursing, and she came immediately to help. I found her coming to help me to be "very romantic".

Our visits to one another increased and progressed to evening meals with wine. We were surprised to discover that we had a lot in common, especially when it came to taste, for example, we had exactly the same televisions, the same cutlery and our furniture was the same or similar. It was all-the-more amazing because our apartments where side by side, whether I was in Eva's apartment or she was at mine, it felt like home.

When you "fall in love" life takes on a whole new meaning. One begins to look forward and make plans. Eva and I decided to live together and after much searching we found a really cool maisonette. We moved in on the 22nd of October 2005 and began our new life together. And for our new home we did not have to buy anything, because most of what we owned was exactly the same so we had double of what we needed, plates cups knives folks, you name it.

Five years later a friend mentioned the story of how Eva and I had met to the local newspaper "Ulricehamns Tidning". The newspaper found our story interesting and asked if they may write an article on how we met. Thinking this to be fun we agreed. To our surprise, on the 21st October 2010, our story became front-page news. Then in 2011 we were approached by two of Sweden's national magazines "Året Runt" and "Hemmets Journal", who also published our story. But that wasn't the end of it; Swedish Radio called and interviewed us as well. To be honest, Eva and I have not fully understood as to why there has been so much interest in our love story. But we find it refreshing to know that we are not the only ones who still love a little romance. Eva and I Married on the 15th of March 2008.

# Chapter 24

## *New Songs and Politics*

Needing something positive to think about whilst working in the factory I decided to carry on writing songs and to stop criticizing politicians and become one myself. Having always had a strong interest in current affairs and politics I decided to join a political party. But which party to join was not an easy decision to make. There wasn't any political party that really reflected my views, each of them had something I agreed with as well as polices that I did not. After much research, the party that I was most in agreement with at the time was the Moderate Party (The Swedish Conservative Party). A general election was to be held in 2006. I put my name forward as a candidate and have since been an elected representative on the local council. After the election in 2014 I was elected to be a representative for the wider region of West Sweden. Being in politics has broadened my horizons, and as with everything we do in life we grow. But one thing is for sure; I have learnt that in politics that the one qualification one needs to have is a lot of patience.

Then I decided to join another organization. I was thinking back over my life's experience, the ups and downs I had gone through, but in the big picture I could see that life had been good to me, so I asked myself the question as to how I might be able to give something back. That chance came when I became a member of the local Lions Club, which is a part of Lions Clubs International. In Lions we raise money across the globe to help people in need, locally, nationally and internationally.

But it always comes back to music. Thanks to the internet it has become easier for song writers such as myself to get our music out, no longer do we have to wait and see if someone at a recording company might be willing to take a chance on our creative work. So, with the new opportunity I set about trying to find a way of transferring songs I had on tape to the new digital system. One of my son's, Sebastian, who is in the music business, put me in contact with someone who could help; at the same time I once again began to compose new songs.

# Chapter 25

## Feel the Love

I was soon to celebrate my 60th birthday and wanted to celebrate in a big way. I asked Eva if she would like to join me on a trip to the US. It had always been an ambition of mine to once again meet my dear friend Chip, and a better birthday present I could not wish for.

Happily Eva agreed to come with me, so on Sept 8th, 2011; we set off for a three-week holiday. We flew to San Francisco, Then having checked in to our hotel I called Chip and we made plans to meet. The excitement and emotion I felt of being reunited with my dear friend after so many years is difficult for me to put into words, but I will try. In fact the only way to describe my feelings was that I was emotionally overwhelmed with anticipation as I waited with Eva on Justin Herman Plaza, which is located at the bay area in San Francisco. "Is that him?", I said to Eva, or "no, there is Chip", then as the man I thought was Chip came closer I realized that it was not him, "where is he?", I said, "he's late"! But then there in the distance, "that's him" I said excitedly to Eva, "Look, the guy with the beard, that's Chip". We approached one another with the biggest of smiles on our faces that you can imagine and then we hugged one another intensely; a passing stranger may have thought that we were two men in love! Then, after a moment or two, I introduced Chip to Eva, and the three of us went to a wine bar and enjoyed catching up on old times, talking mostly about when we, as young teens, had played music together. Although it had been decades since Chip and I last met, it seemed as though five minutes had passed since we were last together.

The following day Chip, together with his wife June, came to meet Eva and I in the City. With our two guides we took a walk and got to see some of the tourist attractions such as Fisherman's Wharf and Pier 39, where we enjoyed seeing the sea lions. We then finalized our plans to stay with Chip and June during the last week of our trip, and looked forward to once again playing the songs we performed as teenagers.

During the following few days Eva and I took a ride on a cable car and stopped off at China Town and then Lombard Street. We also took a long walk in Golden Gate Park. Then we left San Francisco and drove down highway one, from Carmel by the sea to LA. We enjoyed the spectacular and breathtaking views of the Pacific Ocean as we made our way to LA. Here we met another of my lifelong friends, her name is Marion, and the last time we had met was in 1968, whilst working together as models and on television programs in England.

After two nights in LA we drove to Palm Springs and then to the Grand Canyon. On Sept 22nd I celebrated my 60th birthday as we drove through Death Valley, after which we stayed in a hotel at a place called One Pine. The next day we continued our drive to Yosemite National Park. On route we took a photograph that became the album photo for my record *"White Lines" (on the road)*.

The next day we arrived at Chip and June's home in the City of Pleasanton (a suburb of San Francisco). Chip and June, wanting to show us more of the area, took us to Muir Woods and the Golden Gate Bridge. But the highlight of our stay was playing music once again, together with Chip. We remembered how to play some of the songs from when we were young teenagers in England such as *"Tired of Waiting"* by the Kinks, and *"Mrs. Brown you've got a lovely Daughter"* by Herman's Hermits.

Our time together passed, having said our goodbyes to June; Chip, Eva and I hopped aboard the train known as the "Bart" at Pleasant Hill station. The train was to take Eva and I to the airport, and Chip was to leave us and the train on his way to work. When the time came for him to depart we stood up and hugged, with tears rolling down our faces and this was noticed by a woman sitting nearby who commented that she could "feel the love".

# Chapter 26

## Almost There

Upon returning to Sweden, I returned to my work on the factory floor, whilst at the same time I became more engaged with politics and was elected to be a representative in the local judicial court. This new responsibility gave me equal power to the qualified Judge. I sat together with two other elected members, our role was that of a jury, but all of us, together with the judge, had equal power to make a judgment. My almost five years of duty in court taught me a lot about life. Through my years of experience in show business as well as from my time on the factory floor, I had gained a broad and tolerant view of life, and this helped me in my contributing to make what I hope were fair judgments. My official title in Swedish was "Nämndeman". It is important to mention that jury responsibilities in Swedish courts are non-political, even though one can be nominated to the position via a political party, as I was.

Our local bank, Ulricehamns Sparbank, has no shareholders, so elected representatives from the community have the responsibility for electing board members to the bank, as well as to make sure the bank follows all the applicable rules and regulations. I became an elected representative; known in Swedish as "Huvedman".

# Chapter 27

## Light at the End of the Tunnel

In 2016 I had finally reached the age of 65 and became a pensioner. I am, however, still involved in politics, write books, continue to write songs and accept bookings for DJ work. During 2016 I was booked to play at several weddings.

It may sound strange, but I love getting old, I find life easier to handle with each day that goes by, probably because I become a little wiser.

God has blessed me with five fantastic children, and at last count, seven grandchildren. Each of my five children is gifted with various talents. Apart from their day-time work, for which I am equally proud of each of them, Justin is good at drawing and painting, and he has a strong interest in filming. My daughter Heidi writes music and books; I recommend her book "Dreamscape" for those of you who love to get lost in fantasy. Hans is a good guitar player and has arranged concerts. Both James and Sebastian are talented song writers. Together, with a friend, they wrote the hit song *"Falling"*, which in Sweden has achieved gold status. The song *"Falling"* is performed by Sebastian's group "State of Drama".

Sebastian has now become a sought-after musician and music producer. Thankfully he agreed to help me record some of my new songs, for example, *"There Will Come a Time"*, which I released worldwide in March 2016.

Then one day whilst browsing on the internet, by chance, I noticed that my songs *"White Lines on the Road"* and *"Thank You"* had an entry in the Music Master Pop Singles book of 1975-88. This inspired me to re-release the two songs. With Sebastian's help we up-graded the original version of *"White Lines"*. Then, on July 7th, 2016 I re-released *"White Lines"* and *"Thank You"* worldwide. *"White Lines"* has since been played on several radio stations in Sweden.

I then wrote a new song in 2017 entitled *"Because of You"*, inspired by my love for Eva. Released on the 7th January 2018 and produced together with my son Sebastian. The song has since been played on radio in Sweden.

On the 15 March 2018 Eva and I celebrated our tenth wedding anniversary and to our surprise a journalist called from one of Sweden's national magazines "Året Runt". He asked if his magazine could do a new report on how Eva and I had first met in the washroom. This new article was published on our wedding anniversary. Then shortly afterwards we received a call from another journalist, this time from a national newspaper called "Expressen", and their article was published on the 31st March 2018. I wonder, who will call wanting to make the film?

# Chapter 28

## White Soul

"It is easier for a Camel to go through the eye of a needle than for a rich man to enter the kingdom of heaven" (Mathew 19:24). I have given much thought to this, albeit I am not very rich! So why should this bother me? But then again, that depends on who I am compared with. But in any case, I have thought about how it could be possible to go through the eye of a needle. I have come to the conclusion that it is in fact possible. And this happened in 2018 whilst Eva and I were on a trip to Jordan. For one thing I rode on a Camel in the dessert and that got me thinking about the Camel part, which led me to thinking about the needle part. Then whilst we were visiting the Roman ruins in the city of "Jerash", which is situated north of the capital Amman, I got talking with a man by a restaurant, who was a friend of our Jordanian guide "Yosef". I had remarked on how much I liked our guide Yosef and that I found him to be very spiritual, to which he replied "yes, Yosef has a white soul". Since then it has become my ambition to also have a white soul and I have come to realize that if I can achieve having a white soul that it may be possible to pass through the eye of a needle!

## Chapter 29

### *The End of the Beginning*

To this day I still have great difficulty with spelling. In spite of this, and having no formal qualifications, I have managed to survive in life. It is my hope that through my having shared some of my life's experiences with you, that you will be inspired to have confidence, to live your dream and to never give up.

As they say in India, "everything will be alright in the end, and if it is not alright then it is not the end".

This is not the end.

Just before publication of this book I released a new song with the title "Eyes of Gold" on August the 9th 2019. The song is proving to be my most successful to date! Easy to find on internet!

God bless you,
The Author Richard Hallifax

*This book dedicated with love to my family and friends.*
*Special thanks to my Brother Charles Hallifax for his time and*
*expertise in editing this book.*
*To my Father Frederick Neville Hallifax, who lived from 1925*
*until 2010 and wrote this poem*

"The Tides of Life"

When it all seems we are all at sea
The waters are rough and the wind blows strong
We listen and hope that a message of peace
Will soon come along
The tide runs out and then comes in
So those in despair should never forget
That although the calm comes before a storm
The reverse is true and as smooth as before.
By, Neville Hallifax


*To my Mother Lynette Therese Hallifax who lived from 1927 until*
*2005, and wrote this poem*

"The Gate"
Through the gate we all await
Knowing not whose time will come
Some born poor some born rich
We've all been borne like one
It matters not how we abide
Repent but not to late
For heaven lies not on this side
But far beyond the gate
By Lynette Hallifax

*To my God Daughter Faith, 1981-2010*

Faith was born with Spina bifida and suffered from the most serious form of the condition (Myelomeningocele). Despite this she was courageous, and always managed to laugh whenever we where together. For me I believe that my one and only God daughter is a Saint! "Spina bifida is a birth defect that occurs when the spinal cord doesn't form properly".

*Some people the author admires:*

Mahatma Gandhi. He used non-violent methods to achieve his goals.
Nelson Mandela. Quote, *"everything seems impossible until its done"*.
Greta Thunberg. For her courage with trying to stop global warming and climate change.
Malala Yousafzai. For her courage as well as working for all children to have the right to an education.
The Dalai Lama. Quotes: *"be kind whenever possible. It is always possible"*.
*"Remember that sometimes not getting what you want is a wonderful strike of luck"*.
*"My religion is very simple. My religion is kindness"*.
And finally, a quote by the author:
*"Live is like a good wine that when mature, tastes good at the end"*.
Richard Hallifax

# Table of contents

A short introduction by the author